AN INDEX OF AFRICAN AMERICANS IDENTIFIED IN SELECTED RECORDS OF THE BUREAU OF REFUGEES, FREEDMEN, AND ABANDONED LANDS

Jacqueline E. A. Lawson

HERITAGE BOOKS
2008

HERITAGE BOOKS

AN IMPRINT OF HERITAGE BOOKS, INC.

Books, CDs, and more—Worldwide

For our listing of thousands of titles see our website
at
www.HeritageBooks.com

Published 2008 by
HERITAGE BOOKS, INC.
Publishing Division
100 Railroad Avenue #104
Westminster, Maryland 21157

Other books by the author:

The Harveys - Out Of North Carolina

International Standard Book Number: 978-0-7884-0291-3

ACKNOWLEDGEMENT

For their continuous interest, cooperation, and assistance during this project, my thanks are extended to the Director, Phyllip E. Lothyan, his staff, and the volunteers at the National Archives - Pacific Northwest Branch.

DEDICATION

This publication is dedicated to the memory of James Dent Walker, founder of the Afro-American Historical and Genealogical Society in Washington, D.C., in appreciation of his encouragement and support during the summer before his death in 1993.

TABLE OF CONTENTS

DESCRIPTION OF CORRESPONDENCE WHICH INCLUDED NAMES
LISTED ON <u>INDEX TWO</u> - March 1865 Through May 1866.

Grp No.	DESCRIPION OF GROUP	Letter Received	Ltr No.	On Rl	No.of Names
1	"Negroes on Whitehead Farm near Bernard's Mills, Virginia" who left after being intimidated and threatened.	Jun 1865	K-2	15	24
2	Signers of a petition requesting pay for services rendered while employed at the Quartermaster Depot, Richmond, VA.	Aug 1865	Q-18	16	25
3	"Colored Planters," Working Hands On This (Davis') Bend" who signed a paper certifying satisfaction with the treatment by the Freedmen's Bureau.	Oct 1865	D-6	20	109
4	Signers of a petition to retain lands on James Island, SC.	Dec 1865	D-19	20	104
5	Former slaves of Choctaw and Chickasaw Indians attempting to get their families released from the Indians.	Oct 1865	L-37	21	89
6	Attendees of conventions of "Colored People of Virginia for Equal Rights."	Dec 1865	P-52	23	89
7	Freedmen who received grants of 40 acres of land on Edisto Island, SC.	Jan 1866	S-34	24	25
8	Navy volunteers from the USS Allegheny who were swindled out of all or part of their bounty in August 1864.	Oct 1865	W-16	25	53
9	Freed persons upon whom outrages were inflicted in counties of Kentucky.	Mar 1866	K-80	28	45
10	Freedmen signers of a petition requesting release from arrest of two Bureau officers engaged in cultivation of N.C. plantations.	May 1866	R-82	29	130
11	Signers of affidavits attesting to burning of homes, theft of money and property, physical abuse, and murder by rioting white Memphis,TN, residents.	May 1866	K-235	29	182

AN INDEX OF AFRICAN AMERICANS IDENTIFIED IN SELECTED RECORDS OF THE BUREAU OF REFUGEES, FREEDMEN, AND ABANDONED LANDS

This publication lists names of African Americans that were identified in letters to the Commissioner of the Bureau of Refugees, Freedmen, and Abandoned Lands which was in existence from March 1865 through July 1872.

Because of the varied content of the letters received in the Commissioner's Office, the lists in this publication have been divided into three alphabetical indexes. **Index One** lists those names that were abstracted from letters which each contained fewer than 24 names of African Americans. **Index Two** lists those names that were contained in individual correspondence that included 24 or more names of African Americans, i.e., affidavits, petitions, and special reports. **Index Three** is a list of more than 1000 individuals who were sent out to other states from Washington, D.C., on work contracts - a special request by the Office of the President in April 1866. Each of the three indexes contains its own page numbers.

BACKGROUND

The Bureau of Refugees, Freedmen, and Abandoned Lands (commonly known as the Freedmen's Bureau, and abbreviated as "BRFAL") was established by Congress near the end of the Civil War in March 1865 to take over certain responsibilities previously assumed by the Treasury Department and the military. These included supervising and managing matters relating to refugees from war-torn regions, recently-freed slaves (known as freedmen), and abandoned and confiscated lands and property.

Policies administered and decisions made by the Freedmen's Bureau to assist destitute refugees and freedmen were related to distributing food rations, issuing clothing and medical aid, developing and maintaining schools, setting up shelters - tasks similar to those of the modern welfare system. Some of the major Bureau activities concerning the freedmen also included registration of marriages, guidance in labor contracting, resolution of complaints of mistreatment and abuse, and reuniting family members.

Abandoned property was revitalized for hospitals, schools, living quarters, farms for the needy, and other like purposes.

The Civil War ended in April 1865 with the signing of surrender papers by General Robert E. Lee at Appomattox Courthouse in Virginia. Major General Oliver Otis Howard was appointed Commissioner of the Freedmen's Bureau by President Andrew Johnson in May 1865. Major Howard's staff included an Assistant Adjutant General, an Assistant Inspector General, a Chief Medical Officer, a Chief Quartermaster, and a Chief Disbursing Officer. In addition, there were officers in charge of the Divisions of Claims, Education, and Land.

In the former Confederate states and the border states of Maryland, Missouri, West Virginia, and District of Columbia, Assistant Commissioners were assigned to carry out local tasks, with staff similar to that of the Commissioner.

Originally authorized for one year, the authority of the Freedmen's Bureau was eventually extended through July 1872. Its most active years were 1865 through 1869, at which time the Assistant Commissioners were withdrawn from the individual states. Finally, in 1872, with the disbanding of the Bureau, unfinished tasks were turned over to a newly-established Freedmen's Branch of the Office of the Adjutant General.

The voluminous records of the Freedmen's Bureau are now in the custody of the Washington, D.C., office of the National Archives and Records Service. They are filled with names of thousands of individuals such as displaced land owners, freed slaves, homeless refugees, former soldiers and sailors, early leaders in fights for civil rights, lesser-known politicians, and diplomats. The history of their existence, the stories surrounding their lives, and their connections to the living could be lost forever in the myriad of papers and microfilm without an updated indexing system.

In addition to the Washington, D.C., office of the National Archives, there are branches located in large cities throughout the United States (**APPENDIX A**). The microfilmed and original records stored in the National Archives are utilized extensively by researching students, teachers, attorneys, genealogists, writers, political staff members, and family historians.

The need for an index of Freedmen's Bureau records of African-Americans has been cited by several writers:

Johni Cerny: "Black Ancestral Research," in The Source, A Guide-book of American Genealogy (Ancestry Publishing Company, Utah, 1984, page 582).

Robert Scott Davis, Jr.: "Freedmen's Bureau and Other Reconstruction Sources for Research in African-American Families, 1865-1874," in the Journal of the Afro-American Historical and Genealogical Society, Volume 9, Number 4, Winter 1988, page 171.

Colette J. Amico and Shirley J. Burton: "Freedmen's Bureau Records as a Family History Resource at the National Archives," in Federation of Genealogical Societies FORUM, Vol. 1, No. 32, Winter 1989, page 8.

Moreover, the National Archives itself, in the publication Guide to Genealogical Research in the National Archives, published in 1983 by the National Archives Trust Fund Board, discusses the Freedmen's Bureau records. It states on page 177 of "Records of Black Americans":

*In general, however, the nature and arrangement
of the records and the lack of name indexing precludes
easy access to specific genealogical data.*

The purpose of the indexes in this publication is to make available to the general public, in an easily-accessible format, the names and locations of African Americans who either corresponded with or whose names were included in letters to the Commissioner of the Freedmen's Bureau in Washington, D.C.

These letters and their corresponding registers are preserved in Record Group 105, <u>Records of the Bureau of Refugees, Freedmen, and Abandoned Lands, 1865-1872</u>, and recorded on a total of 74 rolls of microfilm as Publication M752. These rolls of microfilm are available at the twelve branches of the National Archives listed in Appendix A.

FILING METHOD OF FREEDMEN'S BUREAU INCOMING CORRESPONDENCE

The methods used for registering and filing incoming correspondence were more or less uniform. As correspondence came into the Commissioner's office, an abstract of the contents was noted on the back of the first page. The correspondence was then entered, by date of receipt, in registers that were organized alphabetically by the initial letter of the surname or office of the writer. The abstract was repeated in the register as the entry was made.

The correspondence was then numbered consecutively within each alphabetical group. An asterisk (*) under the number in the Register indicated that the letter remained in the Commissioner's file; that is, it was not forwarded to another office for action. It was then filed in the same numerical order as it appeared on the register. The contents of the 74 rolls of microfilm are:

Roll 1: A collective index of the names of individuals and organizations who originated the correspondence which is indexed and registered on Rolls 2 through 12.

Rolls 2 through 12: Each roll reflects a specific period of months and contains the indexes and registers of correspondence received during those months. The indexes note only the names of the originator of the letter and not the names mentioned within the correspondence.

Rolls 13 through 73: Copies of the correspondence, registered in Rolls 2 through 12, which were retained in the headquarters files.

The last roll of this series (Roll 74) is arranged by year and contains letters which were not registered as well as some enclosures which were separated from their letters of transmittal.

PROCEDURES USED TO EXTRACT NAMES OF AFRICAN AMERICANS

This publication is divided into three indexes all based on the first three microfilmed rolls of registers and indexes (Rolls 2 through 4) and the first eight microfilmed rolls of correspondence (Rolls 13 through 30) covering the period of March 1865 to May 1866, with one exception: One report from Roll 33 is included because of the subject matter and the date of occurrence (Memphis riots, April 29 through May 4, 1866). The remaining rolls will be indexed in a subsequent publication.

An asterisk (*) by the printed name or location of an individual indicates the best interpretation of illegible handwriting.

In both the registers and the actual correspondence, where an African American was involved, that individual was distinguished by the mention of his (or her) color, stating his relationship to a "former owner," appending the word freedman to his name, describing him as "contraband," or other obvious terms. Although the race designation of "Colored" or "Col'd" was often used in the indexes, this was found to be an unreliable tool for identification purposes as it was not consistently indicated. Therefore, the first step was to read each register entry (contained on Rolls 2 through 4) to extract names of African Americans.

As indicated earlier, if correspondence remained in the file, an asterisk appeared on the register under the number. If there was no asterisk, and thus no correspondence, the register information had to be relied upon.

Finally, each letter contained in Rolls 13 through 30 was read to extract names that were not mentioned in the registers, and to confirm the race of those that were.

Much of the correspondence consisted of narrative reports that included one or two names of African Americans when describing examples of abuse and other problems. Many of these were quite lengthy, and often the handwriting, spelling, and sentence structure were difficult to decipher on a microfilm reader. For this reason, photocopies of most reports were made to facilitate a more careful review and to extract the complete information required for indexing.

DESCRIPTION OF THE INDEXES IN THIS PUBLICATION

Index One includes those African Americans identified in letters which included fewer than 24 names. The following example of the entry of CHARLES ANDREWS demonstrates Index One:

1. LAST NAME of indexed individual .   <u>ANDREWS</u>
2. FIRST NAME of this individual.   <u>CHARLES</u>
3. RECEIVED - Date (year/month/date) correspondence was received.   <u>1865/70/03</u>

4 -7 LOCATIONS - Two fields each for State and City:
The first is the state and city where the correspondence originated.

GA   Ware County

The second is for any other state and city which might be
mentioned in the correspondence.   GA   Savannah

8. SHEET - Page number of the Register listing the correspondence.

Sht. 127

9. LETTER - Alphabetical letter under which the correspondence
was filed.   F (Fowler)

10. NUMBER - Consecutive number of the correspondence as it was
registered.   5

11. Y or N - (Yes or No) Whether or not correspondence is on the
microfilm.   Y

12. ROLL - Roll number on which the correspondence is
microfilmed, if No. 11 is Y. (See NOTE below.)

Roll 14

13. FROM - Name of the office or person originating the
correspondence.   J.S. Fowler, Chaplain,

33rd USCI

14. RE - A brief description of the purpose or contents of the
correspondence, or identifying information concerning the
indexed person.   +After freedom, abused when
attempting to leave owner

NOTE: If the correspondence did not remain in the Commissioner's file (if No. 11 is "N"), the only reference material in
which the subject's name appeared was the Register - Rolls 2, 3,
and 4.

Although consideration was taken to add a field for
"Action Taken," it was decided impractical, since such action
was sometimes too extensive to abbreviate in an index.

A few of the letters include the name and, occasionally, the
location of the former slave owner and are identified by a plus
sign (+) in the RE (remarks) section, as is shown in the above

example. **APPENDIX B** lists these freedmen and their former owners.

Total number of pages included in each letter is not recorded in this index. In many instances, the correspondence consisted of an extensive report which was not page-numbered. A subject's name may have appeared on only one page of such a report, requiring a review of the entire document in order to locate that name.

As the correspondence which remained in the Commissioner's file was read, it was noted that many of the letters included or consisted of reports, petitions, meetings, or affidavits containing 24 or more names of African Americans in each. For this reason, a separate index, **Index Two**, consolidates these names. A descriptive list of the sources for each name precedes Index Two. The number shown in Column 3 of this index corresponds with the number on the descriptive list. Column 4 gives the location of the individual, if given.

Index Three lists 1,145 names of African Americans sent to work under contracts approved by the Freedmen's Bureau, as reported by the Assistant Commissioner of the District of Columbia. Column 1 is the consecutive number assigned to the individual on the original report as the name was listed. Headings for all columns in Indexes Two and Three are on the first page of each indexed section.

HOW TO OBTAIN COPIES OF THE MATERIAL CONTAINING A SPECIFIC NAME OR NAMES

Copies of letters or of registers concerning any indexed name may be obtained through a request to:

Military Reference Branch (NNEM)
National Archives
Washington, DC 20408

The National Archives charges a per-page copying fee and also has a minimum charge for mail orders. A request should include all of the index citation information. Bear in mind that some of the correspondence may consist of several pages, only one of which may cite the indexed name. Because the responding office will charge for each page photocopied, a request might first be made to determine how many pages the correspondence package includes.

INDEX ONE

AFRICAN-AMERICANS IDENTIFIED IN INDIVIDUAL LETTERS AND REPORTS WHICH INCLUDED FEWER THAN 24 NAMES IN EACH

1   LAST NAME of individual being reported.

2   FIRST NAME of individual being reported.

3   RECEIVED - Date (year/month/date) the correspondence was received.

4 - 7   LOCATIONS - Two fields each for State and City: The first is state and city where correspondence originated; the second is for any other state and city which might be mentioned in the correspondence. (See NOTE below.)

8   SHEET - Register page number listing the orrespondence.

9   LETTER - Alphabet letter under which the correspondence was filed.

10   NUMBER - Consecutive number of the correspondence as it was registered.

11   Y or N - Whether or not correspondence is on the microfilm.

12   ROLL - Roll number on which the correspondence is microfilmed, if No. 11 is "Y". (If No. 11 is "N", the correspondence did not remain in the Commissioner's file, and the only reference material in which the subject's name appears will be the Register - Rolls 2, 3, and 4.)

13   FROM - Office or person originating the correspondence.

14   RE - Brief description of the purpose or contents of the correspondence, or information concerning the indexed person.

NOTE: In order to comply with the space allowed, it was necessary, in several instances to reduce the size of a city by abbreviating it - for example, Washington to "Wash", or by eliminating vowels - for example Savannah to "Svannah,", Washington to "Washngtn" and Northhampton to "Nrthhmptn."

ABBOTT, WESLEY   1866/03/10   VA Culpepper Co.
Sht 333   W 72 Y Roll30   **From** G.Denton Williams
Re: *Assaulted after responding to "jeering" remark.*

ABRAHAM, WILLIE   1866/01/04   VA York Co.
Sht 294   V 6 Y Roll25   **From** O.Brown, Asst.Comm. VA
Re: *Merchant; refuses to pay tax.*

ADAMS, RICHARD   1865/06/10   VA Richmond
Sht 54   B 164 Y Roll13   **From** O.Brown, Asst.Comm. VA
Re: *Witness, EDWARD SCOTT beating*

ALESWORTH, ELIZA   1865/11/01   WV Wheeling   PA Greencastle
Sht 52   B 29 N Roll3   **From** Blackman & Haldeman,Attys
Re: *Sold in Middleton VA with 3 children.*

ALSTON, TOBY   1865/12/22   SC Charleston
Sht 176   S 125 Y Roll24   **From** C.C. Bower, Attorney
Re: *Defendant: breaking a contract - dismissed.*

ANDERSON, D. W.   1866/03/12   DC Washngtn
Sht 357   M 128 N Roll4   **From** A.G. MERRY
Re: *Pastor, 1st Colored Baptist Church, Washngtn.*

ANDREWS, CHARLES   1865/07/03   GA Ware Co.   GA Svannah
Sht 127   F 5 Y Roll14   **From** J.S. Fowler, Chap.,33 USCI
Re: *+After freedom, abused when attempting to leave owner.*

ANDRUM, ANTONY   1866/02/14   GA Svannah
Sht 352   W 46 Y Roll25   **From** ABRAHAM WINFIELD et al
Re: *Petition against miscellaneous "evils."*

ASH, MARY JANE   1865/12/21   VA Prince Edw.Co.
Sht 30   A 134 N Roll3   **From** Adjutant General's Office
Re: *Daughter of ROBERT FRANKLIN.*

BACHAN, JESSE   1866/01/02   VA Sussex Co.
Sht 293   V 2 Y Roll25   **From** O.Brown, Asst.Comm. VA
Re: *Shot without provocation or cause.*

BALT, CHARLES   1866/01/02   VA City Point
Sht 293   V 2 Y Roll25   **From** O.Brown, Asst.Comm. VA
Re: *Strangled without cause by citizens.*

BANION, JAMES   1865/12/04   VA Essex Co.
Sht 322   L 76 Y Roll21   **From** J.H. LAWS
Re: *Member, "Colored People of Middlesex Co.."*

BANKS, FRANCES   1866/02/28   DC Washngtn   Fort Monroe
Sht 142   C 78 N Roll3   **From** C.H.Howard,Asst.Comm.DC
Re: *Requests transportation to Fort Monroe.*

BARBOUR, ESSEX   1866/02/16   DC Washngtn
Sht 140   C 68 N Roll3   **From** C.H.Howard,Asst.Comm.DC
Re: *Unaddressed outrages.*

BARNETT, HENRY   1865/09/20   IL Quincy
Sht 251   Q 21 Y Roll16   **From** Quartermaster General
Re: *Question re using rations for AME church gift to benefactor.*

BARTON, ESSEX   1866/03/27   MD St. Mary's Co.
Sht 99   C 124 Y Roll26   **From** C.H.Howard,Asst.Comm.DC
Re: *Late 30th USCT; assaulted by 4 men, including rebel soldier.*

BAUMGARTINE, EMILY 1866/01/15   VA Augusta Co.
Sht 298   V 28 Y Roll25   **From** O.Brown, Asst.Comm. VA
Re: *Child; hit by stone thrown by policeman.*

BEAN, JOHN   1865/07/24   SC Charleston
Sht 32   B 37 Y Roll13   **From** W.J. Bennett, Bvt Brig.Gen.
Re: *Killed by bayonet by rebel ex-soldiers.*

BELL, BILLY   1865/11/24   ID Green Vale   MS Corinth
Sht 55   B 43 N Roll3   **From** HENRY BELL
Re: *Son of HENRY BELL.*

BELL, HENRY   1865/11/24   IA Green Vale   MS Corinth
Sht 55   B 43 N Roll3   **From** HENRY BELL
Re: *Seeking son BILLY and daughter LERTISTA.*

BELL, JOHN   1866/03/02   MD Baltimore
Sht 329   W 62 Y Roll30   **From** Oliver Wood
Re: *Interfering with agents of Oliver Wood who supplies homes.*

BELL, JOHN   1866/03/13   DC Washngtn
Sht 59   B 91 Y Roll26   **From** JOHN BELL
Re: *Pastor, requests building from Government for a church.*

BELL, LERTISTA   1865/11/24   IA Green Vale   MS Corinth
Sht 55   B 43 N Roll3   **From** HENRY BELL
Re: *Daughter of HENRY BELL.*

BENNETT, FRIDAY   1865/12/22   SC Charleston
Sht 176   S 125 Y Roll24   **From** C.C. Bower, Attorney
Re: *Defendant: Breaking a contract - Acquitted.*

BENNETT, JOSEPH   1865/12/22   SC Charleston
Sht 176   S 125 Y Roll24   **From** C.C. Bower, Attorney
Re: *Plaintiff: Suing for $30 labor - Defendent not liable.*

BENNETT, KATIE   1865/12/22   SC Charleston
Sht 176   S 125 Y Roll24   **From** C.C. Bower, Attorney
Re: *Defendant: Breaking a contract - Banishment/forfeiture.*

BENNETT, PETER   1865/12/22   SC Charleston
Sht 176   S 125 Y Roll24   **From** C.C. Bower, Attorney
Re: *Plaintiff: Damage, false imprisonment - Not unjustifiable.*

BERRY, PLEASANT   1866/01/27   AR (Not Given)
Sht 390   M 60 Y Roll22   **From** J.H. McDonald, Clerk
Re: *Seeking pay due.*

BIDE, ANNA   1866/04/15   NC Greensboro
Sht 249   H 94 N Roll4   **From** William Harrison
Re: *Seeking information about her husband, ANDREW NEWHART.*

BLATON, EDWARD   1865/07/13   MS Natchez
Sht 31   B 33 Y Roll13   **From** EDWARD BLATON
Re: *Petition for Wall Street Baptist Church, Natchez.*

BOND, S   1865/11/04   (Military Cmp)
Sht 53   B 32 N Roll3   **From** S. BOND,Co.I, 19th USCT
Re: *+Property stolen by former master.*

BOULDER, ELDER J.F.   1866/02/16   MS Natchez
Sht 72   B 56 N Roll3   **From** ELDER J.F. BOULDER
Re: *Requests possession of Wall St. Baptist Church. (Also B-33)*

BOWSER, EDMOND F.   1865/10/19   NC Coinjock Brdge
Sht 81   C 14 N Roll3   **From** S.N. Cadiville, owned son
Re: *Son of NANCY BOWSER.*

BOWSER, NANCY   1865/10/19   NC Coinjock Brdge
Sht 81   C 14 N Roll3   **From** S.N. Cadiville, owned son
Re: *+Free woman gave up son, Edmond, to apprenticeship.*

BOYD, SAVORY   1865/12/20   PA Shirleysburg
Sht 231   H 67 Y Roll21   **From** Perry Harris, employer
Re: *Employer wants to retain him.*

BOYD, SCOTT   1865/07/03   GA Svannah
Sht 127   F 5 Y Roll14   **From** J.S. Fowler, Chap.,33 USCI
Re: *After freedom, abused when attempting to leave owner.*

BOYD, TALL   1865/07/03   GA Towns Co. GA Svannah
Sht 127   F 5 Y Roll14   **From** J.S. Fowler, Chap.,33 USCI
Re: *+After freedom, abused when attempting to leave owner.*

BOYLE, RICHARD   1865/05/07   NY Roanoke Is.
Sht 25   B 2 Y Roll13   **From** RICHARD BOYLE
Re: *Teacher: Complains of mistreatment of students.*

BRADLEY, AARON A.   1865/10/30   MA Boston GA Svannah
Sht 5   N 28 Y Roll23   **From** S.W. Parker, Frdmn Aid Soc.
Re: *School teacher, lawyer; made speeches; imprisoned.*

BRANFORD, PETER   1866/02/19   KY Mercer Co.
Sht 287   K 60 Y Roll21   **From** C.F. Fisk, Asst. Comm., KY
Re: *Shot without provocation or cause.*

BRIGGS, ELI   1866/04/26   VA Warrenton DC Washngtn
Sht 77   P 86 Y Roll29   **From** R. Morrow, Asst. AG
Re: *Ill treatment by Bureau agent.*

BRISTER, CYRUS   1866/02/27   GA Svannah
Sht 352   W 46 Y Roll25   **From** CYRUS BRISTER
Re: *Personal fight; no injury. (See ABRAHAM WINFIELD et al.)*

BRITTON, NATHAN   1865/12/06   MS Grenada
Sht 371   M 104 Y Roll22   **From** Stuart Eldridge,AAC
Re: *Complaints of cruelty by employer.*

BRODENBERRY, HARRY 1865/12/04   VA Essex Co.
Sht 322   L 76 Y Roll21   **From** J.H. LAWS
Re: *Member, "Colored People of Middlesex Co.."*

BROOKS, HENRY   1866/01/02   VA Powhatan Co.
Sht 293   V 2 Y Roll25   **From** O.Brown, Asst.Comm. VA
Re: *Struck, threatened to be shot.*

BROOKS, HENRY   1866/02/19   DC Washngtn
Sht 109   D 27 N Roll3   **From** George E.H. Day
Re: *Requests pay - labor for Cols. Tompkins & Hodges.*

BROWN, EMILY   1865/12/21   LA New Orleans
Sht 324   L 84 Y Roll21   **From** A. Baird, Asst. Comm., LA
Re: *applies to settle on Government land.*

BROWN, HENRY   1865/11/10   SC Edisto Island
Sht 70   P 27 Y Roll23   **From** R. Morrow, Asst. AG
Re: *Concerning removal from island lands.*

BROWN, JESSE   1866/02/12   VA Richmond
Sht 310   V 90 N Roll3   **From** H. Neide, Insp. General, VA
Re: *Not paid for building a well.*

BROWN, JOHN H.   1865/05/27   VA Norfolk
Sht 44   B 95 Y Roll13   **From** JOHN H. BROWN, petitioner
Re: *Pastor, St.John Chapel, A.M.E. Church.*

BROWN, PHILLIP   1866/03/27   MD Montgomery Co.
Sht 99   C 124 Y Roll26   **From** C.H.Howard,Asst.Comm.DC
Re: *Assaulted, shot by farmer.*

BROWN, REV. HENRY   1865/09/20   IL Quincy
Sht 251   Q 21 Y Roll16   **From** N.C. Meigs, Quartrmstr Gen.
Re: *Question re using rations for AME church gift to benefactor.*

BROWN, WILLIAM   1865/08/11   MD A. Arundel Co.
Sht 88   D 6 Y Roll14   **From** William Daniel, lawyer
Re: *Witness, burning of Magothy Colored M.E. Church.*

BUCK, REV.ABRAHAM   1866/01/04   GA Svannah
Sht 62   B 2 Y Roll19   **From** AARON BRADLEY
Re: *Witness for AARON BRADLEY.*

BUFORT, SAMUEL   1866/04/30   NC Goldsboro
Sht 257   H 117 Y Roll27   **From** Dan T.Horrell, Farm Owner
Re: *Released from jail to work on farm.*

BURDITT, GABRIEL, PVT1865/07/25   KY Camp Nelson
Sht 129   F 14 N Roll2   **From** John G. Fee
Re: *114th USCT; desires to minister at Camp Nelson.*

BURKS, GEORGE 1865/12/16 DC Washngtn
Sht 29 A 129 N Roll3 **From** Rev.J.R.Shepherd,AFA
Re: *Requests transportation for employment.*
BURKS, H.F.(FEMALE 1865/12/16 DC Washngtn
Sht 29 A 129 N Roll3 **From** Rev.J.R.Shepherd,AFA
Re: *Wife of GEORGE BURKS.*
BURRELL, CHARLES 1866/03/24 VA Richmond
Sht 283 V 184 N Roll4 **From** O.Brown, Asst.Comm. VA
Re: *Back pay from Quartermaster Department.*
BURRELL, DENNIS 1865/12/19 LA New Orleans
Sht 323 L 78 Y Roll21 **From** A. Baird, Asst. Comm., LA
Re: *Arrested for holding an election.*
BURRIS, REV. CALEB 1866/02/15 PA Philadelphia VA Nrthhmptn
Sht 71 B 53 N Roll3 **From** REV. CALEB BURRIS
Re: *Representing Eastern Shore colored people.*
BUTLER, RICHARD 1866/03/27 MD St. Mary's Co.
Sht 99 C 124 Y Roll26 **From** C.H.Howard,Asst.Comm.DC
Re: *Assaulted and beaten in presence of a constable.*
CANN, HORACE 1866/01/26 SC Charleston
Sht 187 S 52 Y Roll24 **From** R.K. Scott, Brig. Gen., SC
Re: *Accused - unlawful possession of horse; evidence not heeded.*
CAPEHARD, HARRY 1866/02/05 NC Roanoke Island
Sht 350 W 36 Y Roll25 **From** THOMAS WHITNEY et al
Re: *Petition: Ration tickets taken away.*
CARR, J. B. 1866/01/27 SC Georgetown
Sht 187 S 54 Y Roll24 **From** I.H. SHECKELFOD
Re: *Petition: Unwilling to sign work contract.*
CARTER, JOSEPH 1866/03/03 VA Front Royal
Sht 319 L 46 N Roll4 **From** John B. Lovell
Re: *Seeks title to a horse. (Also V.5, Q-56)*
CARTER, NORMAN 1866/01/04 VA York Co.
Sht 294 V 6 Y Roll25 **From** O.Brown, Asst.Comm. VA
Re: *Merchant; refuses to pay tax.*
CARTER, TONEY 1866/02/14 PA Connellsville
Sht 223 T 47 N Roll3 **From** John Trader, Auditory Off.
Re: *Return of his son.*
CARTWRIGHT, ANDREW 1866/02/05 NC Roanoke Island
Sht 350 W 36 Y Roll25 **From** THOMAS WHITNEY et al
Re: *Petition: Ration tickets taken away.*
CASWELL, JOSEPH 1866/04/10 DC Washngtn
Sht 31 A 201 N Roll4 **From** C.W. Foster, Asst.Atty Gen.
Re: *Co.I, 33rd USCT; $300 owed from a General.*

CEPHAS, DANIEL   1865/12/19   LA New Orleans
Sht 323   L 78 Y Roll21   From A. Baird, Asst. Comm., LA
Re: *Arrested for holding an election.*

CHAPLIN, SHADRACK   1865/12/22   SC Charleston
Sht 176   S 125 Y Roll24   From C.C. Bower, Attorney
Re: *Plaintiff: Debt - Decree for plaintiff of $5.*

CHILDRESS, HENRY   1865/12/15   TN Springfield
Sht 76   P 54 Y Roll23   From R. Morrow, Asst. AG
Re: *Son of MILES CHILDRESS.*

CHILDRESS, MILES   1865/12/15   TN Springfield
Sht 76   P 54 Y Roll23   From R. Morrow, Asst. AG
Re: *+Agreed to pay for freedom of son already freed.*

CLARK, SIMEON   1865/09/20   IL Quincy
Sht 251   Q 21 Y Roll16   From N.C. Meigs, Quartrmstr Gen.
Re: *Question re using rations for AME church gift to benefactor.*

COHEA, GREEN   1866/02/15   MS Vicksburg
Sht 397   M 94 N Roll3   From S.Thomas,Asst.Comm.,MS
Re: *Seeking compensation for destroyed property.*

COLEMAN, ALICE   1866/03/06   VA Richmond   DC Washngtn
Sht 267   V 136 N Roll4   From O.Brown, Asst.Comm. VA
Re: *Requests support from husband WILLIAM COLEMAN for 2 childrn.*

COLEMAN, ROBERT   1866/02/07   VA Ricmond
Sht 307   V 71 Y Roll25   From O.Brown, Asst.Comm. VA
Re: *Remaining on hand until owners build home for him.*

COLEMAN, WILLIAM   1866/03/06   VA Richmond   DC Washngtn
Sht 267   V 136 N Roll4   From O.Brown, Asst.Comm. VA
Re: *Husband of ALICE COLEMAN.*

CONNOR, CHAMP   1865/10/16   DC Washngtn   VA Fairfax Co.
Sht 48   B 12 N Roll3   From F.B. Brown, Jail Warden
Re: *Accused of stealing cow, with WILLIAM TOMPKINS.*

COOK, G. W.   1865/10/20   VA Norfolk
Sht 83   C 23 N Roll3   From G.W. Cook, Counsel
Re: *Judge applicant for Court of Reconciliation.*

COOPER, SAMUEL   1866/02/06   DC Washngtn
Sht 136   C 50 N Roll3   From SAMUEL COOPER
Re: *Pvt. H Co., 30th USCT; seeking bounty.*

CORWIN, RICHARD   1866/05/05   VA Franklin Co.   PA Pittsburgh
Sht 137   R 75 N Roll4   From Samuel Richardson
Re: *Seeking release from bondage of his 2 sons.*

COTT, REV. A.   1866/04/15   VA Richmond
Sht 183   S 196 N Roll4   From REV. A. SCOTT
Re: *Wants lumber for a church. (Also V-244, 252, 267)*

COTTON, BASIL 1865/10/27 MS Vicksburg
Sht 100 D 6 Y Roll20 **From** Joe E. Davis
Re: *Former servant at Davis' Bend.*
COX, REV. JOHN 1866/01/04 GA Svannah
Sht 62 B 2 Y Roll19 **From** AARON BRADLEY
Re: *Witness for AARON BRADLEY.*
COYT, PRINCE 1866/04/11 SC Georgetown
Sht 221 T 108 Y Roll30 **From** Treasury Department
Re: *On petition for appointment as Steamboat pilot. (H-165)*
CRAWFORD, ANDY 1866/01/15 VA Augusta Co.
Sht 298 V 28 Y Roll25 **From** O.Brown, Asst.Comm. VA
Re: *Living with SAM CRAWFORD.*
CRAWFORD, H. 1865/11/18 GA Thompson
Sht 72 P 35 Y Roll23 **From** R. Morrow, Asst. AG
Re: *Concerning the condition of freedmen.*
CRAWFORD, SAM 1866/01/15 VA Augusta Co.
Sht 298 V 28 Y Roll25 **From** O.Brown, Asst.Comm. VA
Re: *Struck on head with knife.*
CRAWLEY, WARRENTON 1866/01/02 VA Nottoway
Sht 293 V 2 Y Roll25 **From** O.Brown, Asst.Comm. VA
Re: *Tied, whipped because he asked for pay.*
CROMWELL, ELI 1866/02/19 DC Washngtn
Sht 109 D 27 N Roll3 **From** George E.H. Day
Re: *Requests pay - labor for Cols. Tompkins & Hodges.*
CROUCH, JANE W. 1865/09/12 VA Alexandria
Sht 345 O 8 N Roll2 **From** E. Owen, Act. Asst. Supt
Re: *Teacher: Abusive treatment from soldiers (See W-72)*
CURLEY, SPENCER 1865/07/29 VA Woodinville DC Wash.
Sht 63 C 31 N Roll2 **From** CURLEY SPENCER
Re: *Wants son back from former "owner."*
CUSTER, JANE 1866/02/15 DC Washngtn
Sht 332 L 35 N Roll3 **From** James C. Lomax
Re: *Bound out by Captain Sherigan.*
DABNEY, JACOB 1865/12/04 VA Essex Co.
Sht 322 L 76 Y Roll21 **From** J.H. LAWS
Re: *Member, "Colored People of Middlesex Co.."*
DANEILS, GEORGE 1866/05/07 DC Washngtn GA Rome
Sht 335 L 91 N Roll4 **From** W.G. LeSur
Re: *Seeking information regarding mother in Rome, GA.*
DANGERFIELD, MINERVA 1865/10/14 TN Jnesboro
Sht 266 K 15 Y Roll21 **From** C.B. Fisk, Asst. Comm., KY
Re: *RICHARD GRIFFIN witness.*

DANIELS, GEORGE   1865/07/13   OH Springfield
Sht 365   P 71 Y Roll16   **From** R.D.Maissey, Mil.Sec./Pres.
Re: *Requests blind pianist's talents be used for colored people.*

DANIELS, JAMES W.   1865/12/04   VA Richmond   VA Middlesex
Sht 322   L 76 Y Roll21   **From** J.H. LAWS, Conf.Secretary
Re: *Chairman, "Colored People of Middlesex Co.."*

DE LYON, JOSEPH   1866/02/24   GA Svannah   GA Hilton Head
Sht 110   D 34 Y Roll20   **From** JOSEPH DE LYON
Re: *Searching for sister, MARY DE LYON.*

DE LYON, MARY   1866/02/24   GA Svannah   GA Hilton Head
Sht 110   D 34 Y Roll20   **From** JOSEPH DE LYON
Re: *Sister of JOSEPH DE LYON.*

DEAN, JOSEPH   1866/03/16   VA Richmond
Sht 277   V 164 N Roll4   **From** O.Brown, Asst.Comm. VA
Re: *Co.O, 2nd USCC; receipt for discharge papers.*

DENNIS, PARRIS   1866/01/27   SC Georgetown
Sht 187   S 54 Y Roll24   **From** I.H. SHECKELFOD
Re: *Petition: Unwilling to sign work contract.*

DICKEY, FLANDERS   1865/10/27   MS Vicksburg
Sht 100   D 6 Y Roll20   **From** Joe E. Davis
Re: *Former servant at Davis' Bend.*

DIGGS, JORDAN   1866/03/27   MD Prince Geo.Co.
Sht 99   C 124 Y Roll26   **From** C.H.Howard,Asst.Comm.DC
Re: *Four children bound to his old master against his consent.*

DIXON, AGNES   1866/02/19   DC Washngtn   MS
Sht 346   A 99 N Roll3   **From** W.A. Nichols, Asst.Adj.Gen.
Re: *+Property bequest from former owner, Martha E. Terrell.*

DIXON, MARGARET   1866/02/19   DC Washngtn   MS
Sht 346   A 99 N Roll3   **From** W.A. Nichols, Asst.Adj.Gen.
Re: *Property bequest from former owner, Martha E. Terrell.*

DIXON, MARTHA   1866/02/19   DC Washngtn   MS
Sht 346   A 99 N Roll3   **From** W.A. Nichols, Asst.Adj.Gen.
Re: *Property bequest from former owner, Martha E. Terrell.*

DODSON, MANUEL   1866/02/27   VA Richmond
Sht 316   V 116 Y Roll25   **From** O.Brown, Asst.Comm. VA
Re: *Requests payment for services in July 1865.*

DORSEY, JOHN   1866/01/10   DC Washngtn
Sht 97   C 6 N Roll3   **From** J.Fullerton,Asst.Comm.DC
Re: *+Sold in 1861; former owner seeks payment.*

DORSEY, JOHN   1866/05/16   DC Washngtn
Sht 115   C 170 N Roll4   **From** W.W. Rogue, Act. Asst.AG
Re: *+Former master demands balance due for child's freedom.*

DORSEY, SARAH ANN 1866/05/16 DC Washngtn
Sht 115   C 170 N Roll4   **From** W.W. Rogue, Act. Asst.AG
Re: +Daughter of JOHN DORSEY.
DRYDEN, ELISHA 1865/08/30 MD (Not Given)
Sht 179   H 34 N Roll2   **From** MARY HARVEY
Re: Has 2 children of MARY HARVEY.
DUTTON, JOHN B. 1865/08/11 VA Waterford
Sht 88   D 7 N Roll2   **From** JOHN B. DUTTON
Re: Wants vacant houses for the benefit of colored people.
EARLY, MILLER 1866/01/15 VA Lynchburg
Sht 298   V 28 Y Roll25   **From** O.Brown, Asst.Comm. VA
Re: Assaulted a white boy.
EDWARDS, DICK 1866/02/14 GA Svannah
Sht 352   W 46 Y Roll25   **From** ABRAHAM WINFIELD et al
Re: Petition against miscellaneous "evils."
EDWARDS, H. 1866/02/14 GA Svannah
Sht 352   W 46 Y Roll25   **From** ABRAHAM WINFIELD et al
Re: Petition against miscellaneous "evils."
ELDER, MILLER 1866/01/15 VA Lynchburg
Sht 298   V 28 Y Roll25   **From** O.Brown, Asst.Comm. VA
Re: Killed by gun shot.
ELMORE, THOMAS 1866/03/13 GA Svannah
Sht 165   S 134 Y Roll29   **From** R. Scott, Brig. General
Re: Deceased soldier; back-pay for family.
EPPS, HARRIETT 1866/01/02 VA Petersburg
Sht 293   V 2 Y Roll25   **From** O.Brown, Asst.Comm. VA
Re: Struck with whip.
EVANS, DOCTOR 1865/11/15 VA Richmond
Sht 18   A 83 N Roll3   **From** Patrick Henry Aylett
Re: Son of JERRY EVANS.
EVANS, JERRY 1865/11/15 VA Richmond
Sht 18   A 83 N Roll3   **From** Patrick Henry Aylett
Re: +Looking for son, DOCTOR EVANS.
EWING, RIDLEY 1865/05/29 KY Owensboro
Sht 281   M 2 Y Roll16   **From** John J. McFarland, neighbor
Re: Fugitive slave; did not enlist in army.
FERGUSON, DELPHEY 1866/05/23 AL Opelika
Sht 205   S 262 N Roll4   **From** John A. Small
Re: Being sought by father, JAMES FERGUSON.
FERGUSON, JAMES 1866/05/23 AL Apelika
Sht 205   S 262 N Roll4   **From** John A. Small
Re: Looking for daughters DELPHEY, TUNIUS, and PATSY.

FERGUSON, PATSY 1866/05/23 AL Opelika
Sht 205 S 262 N Roll4 **From** John A. Small
Re: *Being sought by father JAMES FERGUSON.*

FERGUSON, TUNIUS 1866/05/23 AL Opelika
Sht 205 S 262 N Roll4 **From** John A. Small
Re: *Being sought by father JAMES FERGUSON.*

FIELD, ROBERT 1865/11/10 DC Washngtn VA Petersbrg
Sht 17 A 78 N Roll3 **From** Rev.J.R.Shephard,AFA
Re: *Transportation to Petersburg, VA.*

FINNEY, JORDAN 1866/02/19 KY Walton
Sht 287 K 60 Y Roll21 **From** C.F. Fisk, Asst. Comm., KY
Re: *Family driven from home.*

FISHBURN, HANNAH 1865/10/16 SC Charleston NY
Sht 8 A 36 N Roll2 **From** Rev.S.Abbott, Amer.Un.
Re: *Transportation to Charleston.*

FISHER, MAC 1866/02/17 TN Nashville MO Greenwood
Sht 286 K 59 N Roll3 **From** C.B. Fisk, Asst. Comm., KY
Re: *Robbed and threatened near Greenwood.*

FLOYD, WASH 1866/01/15 VA Lynchburg
Sht 298 V 28 Y Roll25 **From** O.Brown, Asst.Comm. VA
Re: *Threatened lives; assaulted two persons.*

FORD, ISAAC 1866/04/12 VA Richmond
Sht 303 V 234 N Roll4 **From** O.Brown, Asst.Comm. VA
Re: *Requests discharge papers.*

FOWLER, ARMESTED 1866/04/02 TN Nashville
Sht 287 K 95 Y Roll28 **From** C.Fisk,Asst.Comm.,KY/TN
Re: *Tax payer; fined for having a pistol.*

FRAN, RICHARD 1866/02/19 DC Washngtn
Sht 109 D 27 N Roll3 **From** George E.H. Day
Re: *Requests pay - labor for Cols. Tompkins & Hodges.*

FRANKLIN, ROBERT 1865/12/21 VA Prince Edw.Co.
Sht 30 A 134 N Roll3 **From** Adjutant General's Office
Re: *Seeking daughter, MARY JANE ASH.*

FRAZIER, FRANK 1865/07/03 GA Svannah
Sht 127 F 5 Y Roll14 **From** J.S.Fowler, Chap.,33 USCI
Re: *+After freedom, abused when attempting to leave owner.*

FREEMAN, BURRETT 1866/01/02 VA Prince Geo.Co.
Sht 293 V 2 Y Roll25 **From** O.Brown, Asst.Comm. VA
Re: *Tied and whipped.*

FRY, JOSEPH 1865/06/30 DC Washngtn
Sht 127 F 4 Y Roll14 **From** JOSEPH FRY
Re: *Regimental blacksmith seeks payment (Also C-11, Q-7)*

FURBER, ABRAM   1866/02/05   NC Roanoke Island
Sht 350   W 36 Y Roll25   **From** THOMAS WHITNEY et al
Re: *Petition: Ration tickets taken away.*

GAITER, ANTHONY   1866/10/27   MS Vicksburg
Sht 100   D 6 Y Roll20   **From** Joe E. Davis
Re: *Former servant at Davis' Bend.*

GAITER, PHILLIP   1865/10/27   MS Vicksburg
Sht 100   D 6 Y Roll20   **From** Joe E. Davis
Re: *Former servant at Davis' Bend.*

GAITER, SIMON   1865/10/27   MS Vicksburg
Sht 100   D 6 Y Roll20   **From** Joe E. Davis
Re: *Former servant at Davis' Bend.*

GANT, JAMES   1866/02/20   GA Columbus
Sht 225   T 57 N Roll3   **From** H.M. Turner
Re: *Former Co.S, 153rd USCT; shot by a citizen.*

GARCY, JACOB   1865/12/22   SC Charleston
Sht 176   S 125 Y Roll24   **From** C.C. Bower, Attorney
Re: *Defendant: Breaking a contract - Banishment/forfeiture.*

GIBBS, ELIZABETH   1865/06/10   VA Richmond
Sht 54   B 164 Y Roll13   **From** O.Brown, Asst.Comm. VA
Re: *Witness, EDWARD SCOTT beating.*

GIBSON, CALEB   1865/09/01   MS Vicksburg
Sht 468   T 48 Y Roll18   **From** S.Thomas,Asst.Comm.,MS
Re: *Trustee, Fiurst Baptist Church.*

GIBSON, JACKSON   1865/12/28   PA Norristown PA Grdonsvlle
Sht 95   C 88 N Roll3   **From** E.M. Corson
Re: *Wants son, JULIUS GIBSON, returned.*

GIBSON, JULIUS   1865/12/28   PA Norristown PA Grdonsvlle
Sht 95   C 88 N Roll3   **From** E.M. Corson
Re: *13-year-old son of JACKSON GIBSON.*

GILCHRIST, WALTER   1866/04/20   NC Fort Fisher
Sht 343   W 103 N Roll4   **From** Lt. Edwin Williams
Re: *Presents claim for cattle sold to government.*

GILES, JAMES   1865/11/25   NM Rhine Cliff SC Grhamsvle
Sht 283   V 111 N Roll3   **From** Rev. L.B. VanDyke
Re: *+Information on JAMES GILES requested by Rev. L.B. Van Dyke.*

GILES, JOHN   1865/11/29   DC Washngtn SC Columbia
Sht 88   C 50 Y Roll19   **From** John Eaton, Asst.Comm.DC
Re: *Transportation to Columbia with 2 children.*

GILLARD, JOSHUA   1865/10/27   MS Vicksburg
Sht 100   D 6 Y Roll10   **From** Joe E. Davis
Re: *Former servant at Davis' Bend.*

GRANDEE, WILLIAM   1866/02/05   NC Roanoke Island
Sht 350   W 36 Y Roll25   **From** THOMAS WHITNEY et al
Re: *Petition: Ration tickets taken away.*
GRANT, JOHN   1865/12/22   SC Charleston
Sht 176   S 125 Y Roll24   **From** C.C. Bower, Attorney
Re: *Defendant: Larceny - Imprisoned 15 days.*
GRAYSON, ELIAS   1865/10/23   VA Alexandria
Sht 50   B 18 Y Roll19   **From** Joseph Brayer, accuser
Re: *Discharged soldier, accused of passing counterfeit money.*
GREEN, CAROLINE   1865/11/09   DC Washngtn
Sht 362   M 60 N Roll3   **From** Mrs. W.D. Magruder
Re: *Seeking return of children JAMES and CHARLOTTE.*
GREEN, CHARLOTTE   1865/11/09   DC Washngtn
Sht 362   M 60 N Roll3   **From** Mrs. W.D. Magruder
Re: *Daughter of CAROLINE GREEN.*
GREEN, HENRY   1865/10/27   MS Vicksburg
Sht 100   D 6 Y Roll20   **From** Joe E. Davis
Re: *Former servant at Davis' Bend.*
GREEN, HEYWOOD   1865/12/22   SC Charleston
Sht 176   S 125 Y Roll24   **From** C.C. Bower, Attorney
Re: *Plaintiff: Recover a horse - Defendant keep horse; pay $35.*
GREEN, JAMES   1865/11/09   DC Washngtn
Sht 362   M 60 N Roll3   **From** Mrs. W.D. Magruder
Re: *Son of CAROLINE GREEN.*
GREEN, WASHNGTN   1866/04/30   VA Richmond
Sht 317   V 279 Y Roll30   **From** O.Brown, Asst.Comm. VA
Re: *+Killed by former owner.*
GREEN, WILLIAM   1866/04/05   VA Westmorland Co
Sht 131   R 59 Y Roll29   **From** Sarah Richards,Carekeeper
Re: *Elderly, unable to care for himself.*
GREEN, WILLIAM H.   1866/02/05   NC Roanoke Island
Sht 350   W 36 Y Roll25   **From** THOMAS WHITNEY et al
Re: *Petition: Ration tickets taken away.*
GREEN, WILLIS   1865/08/23   OH Madison   VA Page Co.
Sht 65   C 40 N Roll2   **From** S. T. Chase, Judge
Re: *Seeking family in Virginia.*
GREENHOW, ROBERT   1866/01/04   VA York Co.
Sht 294   V 6 Y Roll25   **From** O.Brown, Asst.Comm. VA
Re: *Merchant; refuses to pay tax.*
GRIFFIN, RICHARD T.   1865/10/14   TN Jonesboro
Sht 266   K 15 Y Roll21   **From** C.B. Fisk, Asst. Comm., KY
Re: *Feet amputated. (Also W-51)*

GROSE, JOHN 1865/09/04 MD Charles Co. DC Washngtn
Sht 66 C 48 N Roll2 **From** James Conway, Foreman
Re: *+Driven off plantation while visiting his mother.*
GUILFORD, RICHARD 1866/01/02 VA Brunswick Co.
Sht 293 V 2 Y Roll25 **From** O.Brown, Asst.Comm. VA
Re: *Shot for trivial offense.*
HACKETT, GEORGIANNA 1866/02/09 PA Philadelphia MD Kent Co.
Sht 108 D 21 Y Roll20 **From** Henry M. Dickert, Atty
Re: *Daughter of WILLIAM H. HACKETT*
HACKETT, WILLIAM H. 1866/02/09 PA Philadelphia MD Kent Co.
Sht 108 D 21 Y Roll20 **From** Henry M. Dickert, Atty
Re: *+Daughter, nephew retained by force in Kent Co..*
HAGAN, FLESIA 1866/03/13 FL Tallahassee
Sht 161 F 68 Y Roll27 **From** T.W. Osborn, Colonel
Re: *School teacher (in district operations report).*
HALL, CALVERT 1865/07/25 MD St. Mary's Co.
Sht 343 O 2 N Roll2 **From** E.F. O'Brien, Vets Bureau
Re: *Assaulted, beaton by releasee from prison.*
HALL, JOHN 1865/09/07 KS Osage Co.
Sht 511 W 60 N Roll2 **From** George H. Woods
Re: *+Being sought by son, PETER HALL.*
HALL, PETER 1865/09/07 KS Osage Co.
Sht 511 W 60 N Roll2 **From** George H. Woods
Re: *Son of JOHN HALL; parents being sought.*
HALLEY, AMANDA E. 1886/04/26 VA Warrenton DC Washngtn
Sht 77 P 86 Y Roll29 **From** R. Morrow, Asst. AG
Re: *Ill treatment by Bureau agent.*
HALLING, JAMES 1865/07/20 DC Washngtn
Sht 6 A 30 N Roll2 **From** N.M.Ambrose,Mil.Relief Agt
Re: *C,20th USCT; asks commutation of rations while imprisoned.*
HANDY, JOSEPH A. 1865/05/27 VA Norfolk VA Portsmouth
Sht 44 B 95 Y Roll13 **From** JOHN H. BROWN,petitioner
Re: *Pastor, Emmanuel A.M.E. Church, Portsmouth.*
HANDY, MRS. JOHN 1865/10/30 MD Annapolis
Sht 158 S 35 N Roll3 **From** Rev. Samuel Sawyer
Re: *+Seeks 5 children bound to her former master.*
HANNAH, HENRY 1865/06/03 KY Greenville
Sht 173 H 5 N Roll2 **From** F. B. Hancock
Re: *+Wants to visit his 2 sons "belonging to" Mr.& Mrs. Clarke.*
HARNEY, R. H. 1865/12/22 SC Charleston
Sht 176 S 125 Y Roll24 **From** C.C. Bower, Attorney
Re: *Plaintiff: Owed $122 for wood - Claim disallowed.*

HARRIS, JOHN   1865/11/08 TN Nashville MO Kansas City
Sht 17   A 77 Y Roll19   **From** F.W.Taggard, Asst.Adj.Gen.
Re: *Deceased "contraband:" Inventory of effects.*

HARRIS, MADISON   1865/11/29 NC Concord MD Baltimore
Sht 367   M 84 Y Roll22   **From** W.P.Nelson, M.D.,Asst.Com
Re: *Transportaton to rejoin famiy in Concord, NC.*

HARRIS, MARY   1865/11/08 TN Nashville MO Kansas City
Sht 17   A 77 Y Roll19   **From** Surgeon, Cumberland Hosp.
Re: *Sister of JOHN HARRIS.*

HARRIS, RICHARD   1866/02/17 TN Nashville MO Greenwood
Sht 286   K 59 N Roll3   **From** C.B. Fisk, Asst. Comm., KY
Re: *Robbed and threatened near Greenwood.*

HARRIS, RUBEN   1866/03/20 TN Nashville KY Lyon Co.
Sht 285   K 85 Y Roll28   **From** C.B. Fisk, Major General
Re: *+Whipped to death by former owner.*

HARRISON, H. F.   1865/09/12 VA Aurelia Co.
Sht 180   H 36 N Roll2   **From** H.F. HARRISON, et al
Re: *Petition for assistance to gather crops.*

HARVEY, MARY   1865/08/30 MD (Not Given)
Sht 179   H 34 N Roll2   **From** MARY HARVEY
Re: *Wants children returned from ELISHA DRYDEN.*

HEALSEY, BALAM   1866/01/06 NC Wilmington
Sht 381   M 11 N Roll3   **From** John McRae
Re: *Age 8-10; sought by John McRae.*

HEARD, WILLIAM   1865/12/15 MS Vicksburg
Sht 374   M 117 Y Roll22   **From** S.Thomas,Asst.Comm.,MS
Re: *Threatened if he builds on his rented property. (Also D-78)*

HENDERSON, ANN   1866/03/19 LA Natchitoches
Sht 239   H 62 Y Roll27   **From** W.C.Henderson,BRFAL Agt
Re: *+Agreement with former master/common-law husband.*

HENDERSON, ERLINE   1866/04/12 WV Fairfax MS Linden
Sht 249   H 92 N Roll4   **From** J. Hawxhurst, Post Master
Re: *Seeking return of son, JAMES HENDERSON.*

HENDERSON, JAMES   1866/04/12 MS Linden WV Fairfax
Sht 249   H 92 N Roll4   **From** J. Hawxhurst, Post Master
Re: *Mother ERLINE HENDERSON seeking his return.*

HENDERSON, JOHN   1866/05/22 VA Vienna GA
Sht 137   R 80 N Roll4   **From** J.W. Ross, Capt, 107 USCI
Re: *Late 107th USCI; seeks wife in Georgia.*

HENDSON, JANUARY   1865/11/20 GA Macon MS Macon
Sht 86   C 39 N Roll3   **From** Thomas W. Conner
Re: *+Transportation to Macon MS; seeking wife and 3 children.*

HENSON, THOMAS   1865/10/17   MD Prnce Geo.Co.
Sht 221   H 17   Y Roll21   **From** Clement Hill
Re: *Requests payment for services (9 y.o. in 1850)*
HERNDON, ANNA   1865/11/07   DC Washngton   VA Frdricksbrg
Sht 85   C 35   Y Roll19   **From** John Eaton, Asst.Comm.DC
Re: *Transportation to Fredricksbrg; seeking husband.*
HERNDON, REV. MR.   1865/08/03   DC Washngtn
Sht 71   C 77   Y Roll14   **From** W. Coppinger, Coloniz.Soc.
Re: *Requests transp. to Africa to grandfather's nativity.*
HILL, ELVIRA   1865/12/22   SC Charleston
Sht 176   S 125   Y Roll24   **From** C.C. Bower, Attorney
Re: *Defendant: Breaking a contract - Banishment/forfeiture.*
HILL, NICHOLAS   1866/02/06   VA Richmond
Sht 306   V 66   Y Roll25   **From** O.Brown, Asst.Comm. VA
Re: *Co. F, 39th USCT; bounty due.*
HIMDON, JOHN ZACH.   1866/05/31   VA Lynchburg
Sht 355   W 142   N Roll4   **From** Senator W.T. Willey
Re: *Seeking wife and children.*
HINSON, FRISBY   1865/11/17   PA Erwina
Sht 339   W 33   N Roll3   **From** B.F. Wagner
Re: *+Former master refuses to give up his children.*
HINSON, SANDY   1866/03/27   MD Prince Geo.Co
Sht 99   C 124   Y Roll26   **From** C.H.Howard,Asst.Comm.DC
Re: *Threatened with violence by man holding his daughter.*
HINSON, THOMAS   1865/09/28   MD Baltimore
Sht 182   H 46   N Roll2   **From** THOMAS HINSON
Re: *Sister-in-law wants to leave; brother threatens her (See H11*
HOLLEY, DANIEL   1865/07/13   MS Natchez
Sht 31   B 33   Y Roll13   **From** EDWARD BLATON
Re: *Petition for Wall St. Baptist Church, Natchez.*
HOLMES, DUNCAN   1866/05/21   NC Wilmington
Sht 313   H 135   Y Roll27   **From** DUNCAN HOLMES
Re: *Indicted for "larceny" of his own property.*
HOMES, MARIE   1866/04/17   NC (Not Given)   VA Richmond
Sht 303   V 239   N Roll4   **From** O.Brown, Asst.Comm. VA
Re: *Requests sister, MARY SKIPWITH, from NC. (Also V-322)*
HOPKINS, ROBERT   1865/09/28   VA Alexandria
Sht 223   H 23   N Roll3   **From** P.H. Hambrick, Prov. Judge
Re: *Breach of promise - FANNIE WILLIAMS.*
HOWARD, DENNIS   1865/11/16   MD Sandy Springs
Sht 163   S 59   N Roll3   **From** Jane Schooley, Caretaker
Re: *Caretaker seeks to send HOWARD DENNIS to Freedmen's Home.*

HOWARD, DENNIS   1866/03/24   VA Richmond
Sht 283   V 184   N Roll4   **From** O.Brown, Asst.Comm. VA
Re: *Back pay from Quartermaster Department.*
HOWARD, M.   1866/04/21   MS Fayette
Sht 253   H 104   Y Roll27   **From** M. HOWARD
Re: *Requests Freedmen schools; protection for colored people.*
HOWE, AARON   1866/01/19   NC Wilmington   NC Raleigh
Sht 15   N 11   Y Roll23   **From** E.Whittlesey,Asst.Comm.NC
Re: *Seeing children SOLOMON, ELIZA, and HUNTER.*
HUBERT, S. G.   1865/07/18   PA Philadelphia
Sht 189   H 95   Y Roll15   **From** S.G. HUBERT
Re: *Applies for BRFAL clerkship.*
HURBURT, WILLIAM   1865/08/22   DC Washngtn
Sht 88   D 10   N Roll2   **From** Mrs. S.E. Draper
Re: *Ex-soldier seeks payment for military duty.*
HUTCHINSON, HENRY   1866/03/27   MD Prince Geo.Co.
Sht 99   C 124   Y Roll26   **From** C.H.Howard,Asst.Comm.DC
Re: *Assaulted; now jailed. Wife MARIA HUTCHINSON.*
HUTCHINSON, MARIA   1866/03/27   MD Prince Geo.Co.
Sht 99   C 124   Y Roll26   **From** C.H.Howard,Asst.Comm.DC
Re: *Husband HENRY HUTCHINSON assaulted, now jailed.*
HUTCHINSON, R. K.   1866/05/16   NY New York
Sht 311   H 132   Y Roll27   **From** R.K. HUTCHINSON
Re: *Applying for a position with the Bureau.*
HUTTEN, ELIZA   1866/01/19   NC Lynchburg
Sht 15   N 11   Y Roll23   **From** E.Whittlesey,Asst.Comm.NC
Re: *Daughter of HARRIETT HUTTEN and AARON HOWE.*
HUTTEN, HARRIETT   1866/01/19   NC Lynchburg
Sht 15   N 11   Y Roll23   **From** E.Whittlesey,Asst.Comm.NC
Re: *+Mother of AARON HOWE's children.*
HUTTEN, HUNTER   1866/01/19   NC Lynchburg
Sht 15   N 11   Y Roll23   **From** E.Whittlesey,Asst.Comm.NC
Re: *Son of HARRIETT HUTTEN and AARON HOWE.*
HUTTEN, SOLOMON   1866/01/19   NC Lynchburg
Sht 15   N 11   Y Roll23   **From** E.Whittlesey,Asst.Comm.NC
Re: *Son of HARRIETT HUTTEN and AARON HOWE.*
INGRAHAM, JAMES H.   1865/06/02   LA New Orleans
Sht 147   G 2   Y Roll15   **From** S.A. Hurlbut, Gulf Dept.
Re: *Resolutions concerning conditions of Freedmen.*
JACKSON, A. J.   1866/01/27   SC Georgetown
Sht 187   S 54   Y Roll24   **From** I.H. SHECKELFOD
Re: *Petition: Unwilling to sign work contract.*

JACKSON, ABRAM   1865/08/22   VA Richmond   NY Elmira
Sht 226   J 10 N Roll2   **From** ABRAM JACKSON
Re: *Seeking wife, MINNIE JACKSON.*
JACKSON, JAMES WM.   1866/04/01   DC Washngtn   VA Front Royal
Sht 367   M 161 N Roll4   **From** Tufts Gardner, Agent
Re: *Child of LOUIS and MARGARET JACKSON.*
JACKSON, LOUIS   1866/04/01   DC Washngtn   VA Front Royal
Sht 367   M 161 N Roll4   **From** Tufts Gardner, Agent
Re: *Father of ROBERT and JAMES WM. JACKSON (wife, MARGARET).*
JACKSON, MARGARET   1866/04/01   DC Washngtn   VA Front Royal
Sht 367   M 161 N Roll4   **From** Tufts Gardner, Agent
Re: *Mother of ROBERT and JAMES WM. JACKSON (husband LOUIS).*
JACKSON, MARY ANN   1866/01/15   VA Augusta Co.
Sht 298   V 28 Y Roll25   **From** O.Brown, Asst.Comm. VA
Re: *Man she lives with beats her children.*
JACKSON, MINNIE   1865/08/22   VA Richmond
Sht 226   J 10 N Roll2   **From** ABRAM JACKSON
Re: *Sought by husband, ABRAM JACKSON. (Also B-45)*
JACKSON, PARRIS   1866/04/26   VA Warrenton   DC Washngtn
Sht 77   P 86 Y Roll29   **From** R. Morrow, Asst. AG
Re: *Ill treatment by Bureau agent.*
JACKSON, RICHARD   1866/04/26   VA Warrenton   DC Washngtn
Sht 77   P 86 Y Roll29   **From** R. Morrow, Asst. AG
Re: *Ill treatment by Bureau agent.*
JACKSON, ROBERT   1866/04/01   DC Washngtn   VA Front Royal
Sht 367   M 161 N Roll4   **From** Tufts Gardner, Agent
Re: *Child of LOUIS and MARGARET JACKSON.*
JACKSON, WILLIS   1866/04/26   VA Warrenton   DC Washngtn
Sht 77   P 86 Y Roll29   **From** R. Morrow, Asst. AG
Re: *Ill treatment by Bureau agent.*
JACOX, ALBERT   1866/03/15   DC Washngtn   NC
Sht 139   E 19 N Roll4   **From** Richard Delafield, Maj.Gen.
Re: *Claims pay for services as laborer.*
JAMES, FRANK   1865/06/15   NC Roanoke Is   VA Ft Monroe
Sht 225   J 4 N Roll2   **From** FRANK JAMES
Re: *Co.C, 36 USCT; family not taken care of as promised.*
JAMES, ROBERT   1865/12/06   MS Yazoo Co.
Sht 371   M 105 Y Roll22   **From** Stuart Eldridge,AAC
Re: *Affidavit concerning "disturbed" state of Co..*
JEFFERSON, DAVID   1866/02/01   KY Louisville
Sht 255   J 8 N Roll3   **From** DAVID JEFFERSON
Re: *Co. B, 72nd USCT: Loaned $45 to a captain.*

JENKINS, RANDAL   1866/03/20   VA Tappahannock
Sht 93   C 107 N Roll4   **From** R. Croxton, Attorney
Re: *Claims for wages.*
JOHNSON, HENRY   1865/07/13   MS Natchez
Sht 31   B 33 Y Roll13   **From** EDWARD BLATON
Re: *Petition for Wall St. Baptist Church, Natchez.*
JOHNSON, HOWARD   1866/01/15   VA Shenandoah Co.
Sht 298   V 28 Y Roll25   **From** O.Brown, Asst.Comm. VA
Re: *Tied, shot by man taking him to jail.*
JOHNSON, JAMES ERNEST   1866/03/15   WV Parkersburg
Sht 167   S 146 N Roll4   **From** S.G. Shaw
Re: *Being sought by S.G. Shaw.*
JOHNSON, LEWIS   1866/04/17   VA Richmond
Sht 303   V 238 Y Roll30   **From** O.Brown, Asst.Comm. VA
Re: *No receipt given for retained bounty.*
JOHNSON, LLOYD   1865/08/11   MD A. Arundel Co.
Sht 88   D 6 Y Roll14   **From** William Daniel, lawyer
Re: *Witness, burning of Magothy Colored M.E. Church.*
JOHNSON, PATRICK   1866/02/24   VA Richmond
Sht 313   V 102 N Roll3   **From** O.Brown, Asst.Comm. VA
Re: *Trying to collect money loaned to another.*
JOHNSON, PETER   1866/03/20   VA Franklin   VA Sthhmpton
Sht 269   J 23 N Roll4   **From** PETER JOHNSON
Re: *+Wants to remove grandchild from former owner.*
JOHNSON, RICHARD   1866/02/19   DC Washngtn
Sht 109   D 27 N Roll3   **From** George E.H. Day
Re: *Requests pay - labor for Cols. Tompkins & Hodges.*
JOHNSON, SAMUEL   1866/01/27   SC Georgetown
Sht 187   S 54 Y Roll24   **From** I.H. SHECKELFOD
Re: *Petition: Unwilling to sign work contract.*
JOHNSON, WILLIAM   1866/01/23   DC Washngtn   MD
Sht 131   C 24 N Roll3   **From** J.Fullerton,Asst.Comm.DC
Re: *Mule stolen from him in Maryland.* '
JONES, FRIDAY   1866/01/26   DC Washngtn
Sht 17   N 17 N Roll3   **From** E.Whittlesey,Asst.Comm.NC
Re: *Requests $500 loan to continue his farm.*
JONES, HARRY   1865/11/13   AL Huntsville
Sht 339   W 31 N Roll3   **From** L.H. Waters
Re: *Claim against the United States.*
JONES, ISIAH   1866/03/24   VA Richmond
Sht 283   V 184 N Roll4   **From** O.Brown, Asst.Comm. VA
Re: *Back pay from Quartermaster Department.*

JONES, POMPAY 1865/09/08 AK Pine Bluff
Sht 421 S 68 Y Roll17 **From** A. Forbes, San./Clms Agcy
Re: *H Co.Private deceased; mother asking for pay (Also M-34)*
JONES, SAMUEL 1865/10/19 DC Washngtn MD Annapolis
Sht 358 M 41 N Roll3 **From** H.H. McCoy
Re: *Soldier seeking children held by former master.*
JONES, THOMAS 1865/12/22 SC Charleston
Sht 176 S 125 Y Roll24 **From** C.C. Bower, Attorney
Re: *Defendant: Larceny - No evidence.*
JONES, TONEY 1865/07/13 MS Natchez
Sht 31 B 33 Y Roll13 **From** EDWARD BLATON
Re: *Petition for Wall St. Baptist Church, Natchez.*
KELLEY, ANTHONY 1866/02/24 SC Darlington
Sht 354 W 56 N Roll3 **From** P.K. Whitewood, Chaplain
Re: *Requests horse to enable him to travel and preach.*
KELLY, REV. E. 1865/12/11 VA Fredrcksburg VA Richmond
Sht 273 K 48 N Roll3 **From** REV. E. KELLY
Re: *Ejected from 1st-class boat cabin. (Also K-54)*
KELLY, WILLIAM D. 1866/02/15 PA Philadelphia
Sht 286 K 56 Y Roll21 **From** WILLIAM D. KELLY
Re: *Applies for BRFAL employment.*
KELLY, WILLIS 1865/07/03 GA Ware Co. GA Svannah
Sht 127 F 5 Y Roll14 **From** J.S.Fowler, Chap,33 USCI
Re: *+After freedom, abused when attempting to leave owner.*
KETTO, POMPEY 1865/09/01 MS Vicksburg
Sht 468 T 48 Y Roll18 **From** S.Thomas,Asst.Comm.,MS
Re: *Trustee First Baptist Church.*
KING, GEORGE 1865/07/03 GA Svannah
Sht 127 F 5 Y Roll14 **From** J.S.Fowler, Chap,33 USCI
Re: *+After freedom, abused when attempting to leave owner.*
KIRKLAND, CHARLES 1865/07/03 GA Svannah
Sht 127 F 5 Y Roll14 **From** J.S.Fowler, Chap,33 USCI
Re: *+After freedom, abused when attempting to leave owner.*
KIRKLAND, MARTHA 1865/07/03 GA Svannah
Sht 127 F 5 Y Roll14 **From** J.S.Fowler, Chap,33 USCI
Re: *+After freedom, abused when attempting to leave owner.*
KNIGHT, RIGHT 1866/01/27 NC Goldsboro
Sht 17 N 21 Y Roll23 **From** Thos P. Johnson, AAC, NC
Re: *Refused to pay note for owned property.*
LANKFORD, HETTY A. 1865/09/23 MD Somerset MD Burnettsville
Sht 262 L 25 Y Roll15 **From** HETTY A. LANKFORD
Re: *Son, ISASA LANKFORD, being held in bondage.*

LANKFORD, ISASA   1865/09/23   MD Burnettsville
Sht 262   L 25 Y Roll15   **From** HETTY A. LANKFORD
Re: +*Son of HETTY A. LANKFORD, being held in bondage.*

LAUGHLIN, ASBERRY   1865/10/14   TN Jonesboro
Sht 266   K 15 Y Roll21   **From** C.B. Fisk, Asst. Comm., KY
Re: *RICHARD GRIFFIN witness.*

LAWS, J. H.   1865/12/04   VA Essex Co.   VA Middlesex
Sht 322   L 76 Y Roll21   **From** J.H. LAWS
Re: *Secretary, "Colored People of Middlesex Co.."*

LEE, AARON   1866/02/20   MD Mt. Washngtn
Sht 225   T 56 N Roll3   **From** Jane S. Townsend
Re: *Seeking wages due him.*

LEE, HENRY   1866/02/03   VA Richmond
Sht 305   V 63 Y Roll25   **From** O.Brown, Asst.Comm. VA
Re: *Requests back pay due since Emancipation date.*

LEWIS, DR. A.W.   1865/06/02   LA New Orleans
Sht 147   G 2 Y Roll15   **From** S.A. Hurlbut, Gulf Dept.
Re: *Resolutions concerning conditions of Freedmen.*

LEWIS, ROBERT   1866/05/25   VA Yorktown
Sht 367   V 323 Y Roll30   **From** Jacob H.Vining, Frdmn Sch.
Re: *Beaten in court room.*

LEWIS, WILLIAM   1865/10/27   MS Vicksburg
Sht 100   D 6 Y Roll20   **From** Joe E. Davis
Re: *Former servant at Davis' Bend.*

LEWIS, WILLIAM H.   1865/05/27   VA Portsmouth   VA Norfolk
Sht 44   B 95 Y Roll13   **From** JOHN H. BROWN, petitioner
Re: *Pastor, St.Luke's Protestant Methodist Church.*

LITTLE, NANCY   1866/01/02   VA Southhampton
Sht 293   V 2 Y Roll25   **From** O.Brown, Asst.Comm. VA
Re: *Brutally whipped.*

LOUIS, HENRY   1866/04/26   VA Warrenton   DC Washngtn
Sht 77   P 86 Y Roll29   **From** R. Morrow, Asst. AG
Re: *Ill treatment by Bureau agent.*

LUCAS, JAMES   1865/10/12   MI Niles   VA Westmorland Co
Sht 356   M 32 N Roll3   **From** H.H. Morrow
Re: *Seeking information regarding wife, Sarah, in Westmorland.*

LUCAS, SARAH   1865/10/12   VA Westmorland Co
Sht 356   M 32 N Roll3   **From** H.H. Morrow
Re: *Wife of JAMES LUCAS.*

LUCKMAN, JOSEPH   1865/08/11   MD Baltimore   DC Washngtn
Sht 8   A 44 N Roll3   **From** C.W. Foster, Asst. Adj Gen
Re: *30th USCT, seeking bounty.*

LYLES, ANN 1865/12/05 VA Richmond
Sht 170 S 97 Y Roll24 **From** Thadeus Stevens, Senator
Re: *Daughter of JANE LYLES.*

LYLES, JANE 1865/12/05 VA Richmond
Sht 170 S 97 Y Roll24 **From** Thadeus Stevens, Senator
Re: *Requests transp. of children to DC from Richmond. (Also G-21*

LYLES, JERRY 1865/12/05 VA Richmond
Sht 170 S 97 Y Roll24 **From** Thadeus Stevens, Senator
Re: *Son of JANE LYLES.*

LYNCH, NICHOLAS 1865/12/12 VA Richmond
Sht 286 V 127 Y Roll25 **From** O.Brown, Asst.Comm. VA
Re: *Bounty voucher approved.*

MAHON, CHARLES 1866/03/12 VA Richmond
Sht 271 V 148 N Roll4 **From** O.Brown, Asst.Comm. VA
Re: *Co.B, 1st USCC; requests receipt for discharge papers.*

MANN, ALEX 1865/12/04 VA Essex Co.
Sht 322 L 76 Y Roll21 **From** J.H. LAWS
Re: *Member, "Colored People of Middlesex Co.."*

MARTINS, WILLIS 1865/07/03 GA Svannah
Sht 127 F 5 Y Roll14 **From** J.S.Fowler, Chap,33 USCI
Re: *After freedom, abused when attempting to leave owner.*

MATTOX, MOSES 1865/07/03 GA Svannah
Sht 127 F 5 Y Roll14 **From** J.S.Fowler, Chap,33 USCI
Re: *After freedom, abused when attempting to leave owner.*

MC DOUD, REUBEN 1866/04/06 NC Wilmington NC Raleigh
Sht 15 N 90 N Roll4 **From** E.Whittlesey,Asst.Comm.NC
Re: *Received whipping, by Court Order.*

MC GEE, MILLIE 1865/09/25 AR Batesville MO St. Louis
Sht 43 B 90 N Roll2 **From** J.T. Bradley
Re: *Seeks pay for services, Batesville Hospital.*

MC GILFRY, JOHN 1866/02/14 GA Svannah
Sht 352 W 46 Y Roll25 **From** ABRAHAM WINFIELD et al
Re: *Petition against miscellaneous "evils."*

MC GILFRY, T. 1866/02/14 GA Svannah
Sht 352 W 46 Y Roll25 **From** ABRAHAM WINFIELD et al
Re: *Petition against miscellaneous "evils."*

MC KINNAE, RASMUS 1865/12/06 MS Yazoo Co.
Sht 371 M 105 Y Roll22 **From** Stuart Eldridge,AAC
Re: *Affidavit concerning "disturbed" state of Co..*

MC RAE, JOHN 1866/01/06 NC Wilmington
Sht 381 M 11 N Roll3 **From** John McRae
Re: *Age 8-10; sought by JOHN MC RAE.*

MERIDITH, ELISHA   1866/03/26   NY New York
Sht 67   B 112 N Roll4   **From** F.A. Babcock
Re: +*Being sought by F.A. Babcock*

MERRY, A.G.   1866/03/12   TN Nashville   DC Washngtn
Sht 357   M 128 N Roll4   **From** A.G. MERRY
Re: *Pastor, 1st Colored Baptist Church, Nashville.*

MIDDLETON, JAMES   1865/09/01   MS Vicksburg
Sht 468   T 48 Y Roll18   **From** S.Thomas,Asst.Comm.,MS
Re: *Trustee, First Baptist Church.*

MILLAM, ELIAS   1865/08/22   KY (Not Given)   OH Xenia
Sht 89   D 11 N Roll2   **From** Mrs. Mary J. Dallas
Re: *Son of SUSAN MILLAM.*

MILLAM, SUSAN   1865/08/22   KY (Not Given)   OH Xenia
Sht 89   D 11 N Roll2   **From** Mrs. Mary J. Dallas
Re: *Seeks son, ELIAS MILLAM.*

MILLEDGE, GLASCO   1866/02/14   GA Svannah
Sht 352   W 46 Y Roll25   **From** ABRAHAM WINFIELD et al
Re: *Petition against miscellaneous "evils."*

MILLER, HENRY   1865/11/08   NC Raleigh
Sht 6   N 33 Y Roll23   **From** E.Whittlesey,Asst.Comm.NC
Re: *Treatment complaint. (8 pages total)*

MILLER, TAYLOR   1865/12/12   DC Washngtn
Sht 373   M 111 N Roll3   **From** TAYLOR MILLER
Re: *Applies for hotel license.*

MILLS, ELIZABETH   1865/09/20   KY Lebanon   DC Washngtn
Sht 361   P 39 Y Roll16   **From** Joseph Fry, Prov.Marsh.Gen
Re: *Given pass with consent of "master."*

MINER, PATSY   1865/11/07   DC Washngtn   VA Fredricksbrg
Sht 85   C 35 Y Roll19   **From** John Eaton, Asst.Comm., DC
Re: *To accompany ANNA HERNDON.*

MINOR, JANE   1865/06/10   VA Richmond
Sht 54   B 164 Y Roll13   **From** O.Brown, Asst.Comm. VA
Re: *Witness, EDWARD SCOTT beating.*

MINTON, WILLIAM H.   1865/06/12   PA Philadelphia
Sht 291   M 57 Y Roll16   **From** WILLIAM H. MINTON
Re: *Applies for BFRAL clerkship.*

MITCHELL, WILLIAM   1866/04/11   SC Georgetown
Sht 221   T 108 Y Roll30   **From** Treasury Department
Re: *On petition for appointment at Steamboat pilot. (H-165)*

MONTGOMERY, BENJAMIN F.   1865/10/27   MS Vicksburg
Sht 100   D 6 Y Roll20   **From** Joe E. Davis
Re: *Former servant at Davis' Bend.*

MOONEY, SALLIE 1866/05/21 SC (Not Given) NC Raleigh
Sht 27 N 127 N Roll4 **From** E.Whittlesey,Asst.Comm.NC
Re: *Seeking 2 solen children now in South Carolina.*

MOORE, JULIA 1865/09/20 NY Ellington
Sht 53 B 160 Y Roll13 **From** James Boyden, friend
Re: *+Mistreated by employer; Boyden trying to get her release.*

MOORE, SARAH 1866/05/21 DC Washngtn NC Wilmington
Sht 221 G 175 Y Roll27 **From** D.R. Goodloe, U.S. Marshall
Re: *Requests possession of her property in Wilmington.*

MORGAN, JAMES 1865/07/03 GA Clinch Co. GA Svannah
Sht 127 F 5 Y Roll14 **From** J.S.Fowler, Chap,33 USCI
Re: *+After freedom, abused when attempting to leave owner.*

MORGAN, JERRY 1866/02/05 NC Roanoke Island
Sht 350 W 36 Y Roll25 **From** THOMAS WHITNEY et al
Re: *Petition: Ration tickets taken away.*

MORRIS, HENRY 1865/12/06 MS Grenada
Sht 371 M 104 Y Roll22 **From** Stuart Eldridge,AAC
Re: *Complaints of cruelty by employer.*

MORTON, JOHN 1865/07/15 LA New Orleans
Sht 80 C 145 Y Roll14 **From** Thos.Conway, Asst.Comm.LA
Re: *+Locked in "workhouse" under false charges.*

MOULTRIE, ISHMAL 1865/11/10 SC Edisto Island
Sht 70 P 27 Y Roll23 **From** R. Morrow, Asst. AG
Re: *Concerning removal from island lands.*

NELSON, DANGERFIELD 1865/10/14 TN Jonesboro
Sht 266 K 15 Y Roll21 **From** C.B. Fisk, Asst. Comm., KY
Re: *RIGHARD GIFFIN case; husband of MINERVA DANGERFIELD.*

NEWHART, ANDREW 1866/04/15 NC Greensboro
Sht 249 H 94 N Roll4 **From** William Harrison
Re: *Being sought by wife, ANNA BIDE.*

NEWMAN, FRANKY 1866/03/13 KY Barron Co.
Sht 285 K 83 Y Roll28 **From** Samuel Martin, Supt., KY
Re: *+Wants son, MICKY NEWMAN, back from former owner.*

NEWMAN, MICKY 1866/03/13 KY Barron Co.
Sht 285 K 83 Y Roll28 **From** Samuel Martin, Supt., KY
Re: *+Being sought, by mother FRANKY NEWMAN, from former owner.*

NORFLEET, JERRY 1866/04/06 VA Suffolk VA Craney Island
Sht 27 A 188 N Roll4 **From** E.S. Townsend, Asst. AG
Re: *Seeks pay for work at Suffolk & Craney Island.*

NORTON, D. M. 1866/03/30 VA Hampton
Sht 13 N 86 N Roll4 **From** D.M. NORTON
Re: *Goods stolen; seeking proper court trial.*

NOTASH, WILLIAM   1865/08/02   FL St.Augustine
Sht 33   B 41 N Roll2   **From** J.Brinkerhoff, Spt/Freedmn
Re: *Reclaiming horses furnished to Union army; lost requisition.*
OLIVER, JOHN   1866/05/25   VA Richmond
Sht 365   V 319 Y Roll30   **From** O.Brown, Asst.Comm. VA
Re: *Presents resolution to retain present superintendent of VA.*
ORCE, JOHN   1865/12/22   SC Charleston
Sht 176   S 125 Y Roll24   **From** C.C. Bower, Attorney
Re: *Plaintiff: Recover a mule - Mule, or $75 value to Plaintiff.*
OSBORNE, SAM   1865/07/22   VA Danville   MN Waterville
Sht 129   F 11 N Roll2   **From** Stephen C.Fletcher,late Lt
Re: *Seeking wife and child in Danville.*
OWENS, SAMUEL   1866/02/05   NC Roanoke Island
Sht 350   W 36 Y Roll25   **From** THOMAS WHITNEY et al
Re: *Petition: Ration tickets taken away.*
PACK, CHARITY   1865/08/11   MD A. Arundel Co.
Sht 88   D 6 Y Roll14   **From** William Daniel, lawyer
Re: *Witness, burning of Magothy Colored M.E. Church.*
PAINE, WILLIS   1865/10/27   MS Vicksburg
Sht 100   D 6 Y Roll20   **From** Joe E. Davis
Re: *Former servant at Davis' Bend.*
PAPINA, GEORGE   1865/08/02   FL St.Augustine
Sht 33   B 41 N Roll2   **From** J.W.Brinkerhoff, Spt/Freedmn
Re: *Reclaiming horses furnished to Union army; lost requisition.*
PARK, MARY   1865/11/25   VA Richmond   DC Washngtn
Sht 22   A 100 Y Roll19   **From** Am.Freedmen's Aid Comm.
Re: *Transportation to Richmond to be with her mother.*
PARKER, ROSA   1866/01/04   VA Elizabeth City
Sht 294   V 5 Y Roll25   **From** O.Brown, Asst.Comm. VA
Re: *Assaulted in Hampton.*
PARKER, S   1866/01/26   AL Mobile
Sht 81   P 18 Y Roll23   **From** R. Morrow, Asst. AG
Re: *Presents employment plan for freedmen.*
PAULLEY, L. D.   1866/01/27   SC Georgetown
Sht 187   S 54 Y Roll24   **From** I.H. SHECKELFOD
Re: *Petition: Unwilling to sign work contract.*
PENDLETON, GABRIEL 1866/03/19   FL Tallahassee   MD Baltimore
Sht 163   F 74 N Roll4   **From** T.W. Osborn, Colonel
Re: *Transportation from Baltimore to Tallahassee.*
PERKINS, KATE   1866/05/14   MS Vicksburg
Sht 383   M 211 N Roll4   **From** T.J. Wood, Major General
Re: *Seeking information regarding son, BENJAMIN TURNER.*

PERRY, JOHN E.   1865/08/24   TX Dallas   MO Springfield
Sht 36   B 60 N Roll2   **From** S.W. Boyd
Re: *Seeking 6 brothers and sisters, "carried off" in 1862.*

PETERS, CARTER   1865/12/04   VA Essex Co.
Sht 322   L 76 Y Roll21   **From** J.H. LAWS
Re: *Member, "Colored People of Middlesex Co.."*

PETERSON, ANNY   1865/12/04   VA Essex Co.
Sht 322   L 76 Y Roll21   **From** J.H. LAWS
Re: *Member, "Colored People of Middlesex Co.."*

PHILLIPS, T.   1866/01/04   TN Pulaski   MS Wood Station
Sht 345   W 4 N Roll3   **From** Samuel V. Wickard
Re: *17th USCT; bounty and pay.*

PITT, CALEB   1865/08/05   VA Norfolk
Sht 63   C 34 Y Roll14   **From** Mayor Daniel Collins
Re: *Owner of horse and wagon (See STEPHEN WICKS)*

POOLE, LEVI   1866/02/05   NC Roanoke Island
Sht 350   W 36 Y Roll25   **From** THOMAS WHITNEY et al
Re: *Petition: Ration tickets taken away.*

POWELL, BETSY   1865/11/08   NC Raleigh
Sht 6   N 33 Y Roll23   **From** E.Whittlesey,Asst.Comm.NC
Re: *Treatment complaint. (8 pages total)*

POWELL, WILLIAM   1866/04/17   NY Brooklyn
Sht 223   T 112 N Roll4   **From** Lewis Tappan
Re: *Suggested to head Freedmen "employment bureau."*

RAINEY, ELDER L.   1866/01/27   SC Georgetown
Sht 187   S 54 Y Roll24   **From** I.H. SHECKELFOD
Re: *Petition: Unwilling to sign work contract.*

REED, JAMES   1866/04/06   LA New Orleans   DC Washngtn
Sht 27   A 190 N Roll4   **From** E.S. Townsend, Asst. AG
Re: *Transportation for Reed and children from New Orleans.*

REEVES, CALEB   1865/10/24   (Not Given)
Sht 17   R 9 N Roll3   **From** CALEB REEVES
Re: *Recommends S.S.Roby as "friend to the colored people."*

RICHARDSON, ALEXANDER   1866/03/12   VA Richmond
Sht 271   V 148 N Roll4   **From** O.Brown, Asst.Comm. VA
Re: *Co.B, 1st USCC; requests receipt for discharge papers.*

ROBINSON, ELIAS   1865/11/01   AL Huntsville
Sht 17   R 10 N Roll3   **From** ELIAS ROBINSON
Re: *Submits claim for 2 horses seized by government.*

ROBINSON, TOM   1866/05/18   DE Wilmington
Sht 347   W 112 Y Roll30   **From** J.H. Wilmer, Bvt.Brig.Gen.
Re: *Protection for Freedmen's schools.*

ROUSE, NED   1866/04/28   NC Lenoir Co.   DC Washngtn
Sht 257   H 115 N Roll4   **From** J.F. Hardigan
Re: *Murdered by returned rebel soldiers.*

RUFFIN, ROB   1865/12/22   SC Charleston
Sht 176   S 125 Y Roll24   **From** C.C. Bower, Attorney
Re: *Defendant: Action for bedstead - Bedstead to plaintiff.*

RUFUS, CHARLES   1866/04/05   TN Nashville   DC Washngtn
Sht 25   A 185 N Roll4   **From** A.F. Rocknell, Asst. AG
Re: *Transfer to Nashville to secure military history.*

RUSSELL, JOHN H.   1866/03/19   VA Richmond
Sht 279   V 171 N Roll4   **From** O.Brown, Asst.Comm. VA
Re: *To collect money owned by former boarders. (Also V-200)*

RUSSELL, RACHEL   1865/12/22   SC Charleston
Sht 176   S 125 Y Roll24   **From** C.C. Bower, Attorney
Re: *Plaintiff: Personal threats - $50 bond, keep peace 3 months.*

RYALL, FERDINAND   1865/11/06   ME Troy
Sht 338   W 28 N Roll3   **From** Albien Whittier
Re: *+Looking for mother, LOUISA RYALL.*

RYALL, LOUISA   1865/11/06   ME Troy
Sht 338   W 28 N Roll3   **From** Albien Whittier
Re: *Mother of FERDINAND RYALL.*

SACKET, (MISS)   1866/03/30   AR Little Rock
Sht 365   M 156 Y Roll28   **From** J.S. Sprague
Re: *Colored teacher.*

SAMPSON, YATES   1865/11/10   SC Edisto Island
Sht 70   P 27 Y Roll23   **From** R. Morrow, Asst. AG
Re: *Concerning removal from island lands.*

SCOTT, CHARLIE   1866/01/04   VA York Co.
Sht 294   V 6 Y Roll25   **From** O.Brown, Asst.Comm. VA
Re: *Merchant; refuses to pay tax.*

SCOTT, DAVID   1865/09/20   VA Hanover   NY Albany Co.
Sht 20   A 97 Y Roll3   **From** Samuel L. Anabel, employer
Re: *+Employer wants to bring SCOTT family from the south.*

SCOTT, EDWARD   1865/06/10   VA Richmond
Sht 54   B 164 Y Roll13   **From** O.Brown, Asst.Comm. VA
Re: *Severly attacked and beaten for being "colored"*

SCOTT, JINNY   1865/06/10   VA Richmond
Sht 54   B 164 Y Roll13   **From** O.Brown, Asst.Comm. VA
Re: *Wife of EDWARD SCOTT.*

SCOTT, PATRICK   1865/11/30   MD Baltimore
Sht 229   H 53 N Roll3   **From** Wm. H. Hogarth, AG Office
Re: *Wants "papers" returned.*

SCROGGINS, JANE   1865/08/31   AL Greene Co.
Sht 468   T 47 N Roll2   **From** Felix K. Thornton
Re: +Seeking daughter, JUNE SCROGGINS.
SCROGGINS, JUNE   1865/08/31   AL Greene Co.
Sht 468   T 47 N Roll2   **From** Felix K. Thornton
Re: Daughter of JANE SCROGGINS.
SHECKELFOD, I. H.   1866/01/27   SC Georgetown
Sht 187   S 54 Y Roll24   **From** I.H. SHECKELFOD
Re: Petition: Unwilling to sign work contract.
SHELMAN, SANDY   1866/02/14   GA Svannah
Sht 352   W 46 Y Roll25   **From** ABRAHAM WINFIELD et al
Re: Petition against miscellaneous "evils."
SHELTON, ALONZO   1865/09/21   VA Alexandria   MD
Sht 180   H 40 N Roll2   **From** P.H. Hambrick, Prov. Judge
Re: Claim for damage to crop in Maryland.
SHEPPARD, PETER   1865/05/17   VA Norfolk
Sht 44   B 95 Y Roll13   **From** JOHN H. BROWN, petitioner
Re: Minister of the Gospel.
SHORT, GEORGE   1865/12/06   MS Grenada
Sht 371   M 104 Y Roll22   **From** Stuart Eldridge,AAC
Re: Complaints of cruelty by employer.
SIMMS, J. M.   1866/02/14   GA Svannah
Sht 195   S 97 Y Roll24   **From** J. M. SIMMS
Re: Employment abuse.
SIMMS, JAMES M.   1866/05/04   GA Augusta   GA Svannah
Sht 215   G 158 N Roll4   **From** D. Tillson, Brig. General
Re: Desires cemetery for colored people.
SIMMS, REV. J. M.   1865/06/15   GA Svannah
Sht 409   S 15 Y Roll17   **From** REV. J. M. SIMMS
Re: Ill treatment by military authorities.
SIMPSON, PETER   1866/01/26   WV Culpepper
Sht 66   B 29 N Roll3   **From** Mrs. Caroline Bowman
Re: Contract violated by husband of Caroline Bowman.
SIMS, ADELINE   1866/04/26   DC Washngtn
Sht 255   H 110 N Roll4   **From** W.S. Higgins
Re: Owes balance due on a "shanty."
SKIPWITH, MARY   1866/04/17   NC (Not Given)   VA Richmond
Sht 303   V 239 N Roll4   **From** O.Brown, Asst.Comm. VA
Re: Sister of MARIE HOMES.
SMALL, ALFRED   1865/09/29   NC New Bern
Sht 359   P 33 N Roll2   **From** A. Morrow, Asst. Atty Gen.
Re: Seeks permission to peddle in Jamestown.

SMALL, SAMUEL   1865/12/22   SC Charleston
Sht 176   S 125 Y Roll24   **From** C.C. Bower, Attorney
Re: *Defendant: Larceny of rice - Confined for 60 days.*
SMITH, ANSON   1866/05/01   DC Washngtn VA Richmond
Sht 143   E 32 N Roll4   **From** Richard Delafield, Maj.Gen.
Re: *Payment for services at Fort Monroe and Richmond.*
SMITH, CHARLES H.   1866/03/13   VA Lynchburg
Sht 165   S 136 N Roll4   **From** CHARLES H. SMITH
Re: *Seeks justice in a freedmen's court.*
SMITH, VIRGIL C.   1865/11/06   MD Annapolis
Sht 160   S 45 Y Roll24   **From** VIRGIL C. SMITH
Re: *Seeks protection from abuses. (Also D-21 and T-56, 1866)*
SNIPS, STAFFORD   1866/02/14   GA Svannah
Sht 352   W 46 Y Roll25   **From** ABRAHAM WINFIELD et al
Re: *Petition against miscellaneous "evils."*
SNOWDEN, BENJAMIN   1866/02/05   NC Roanoke Island
Sht 350   W 36 Y Roll25   **From** THOMAS WHITNEY et al
Re: *Petition: Ration tickets taken away.*
SPARKS, HENRY   1865/11/10   LA New Orleans
Sht 161   S 60 N Roll3   **From** HENRY SPARKS
Re: *Seeking bounty for military service.*
SPEAKE, RICHARD   1866/03/27   MD St. Mary's Co.
Sht 99   C 124 Y Roll26   **From** C.H.Howard,Asst.Comm.DC
Re: *Assaulted and beaten by employer.*
SPRIGGS, ALEX   1865/12/13   WV Taylor Co.
Sht 173   S 114 Y Roll24   **From** ALEX SPRIGGS
Re: *Suggests taxing colored to buy their own lands.*
STARKE, JANE   1866/04/30   NC Charlottsville
Sht 125   D 64 N Roll4   **From** David Diggs
Re: *Freedmen's Court decision appeal.*
STIENES, LEN   1865/11/08   NC Raleigh
Sht 6   N 33 Y Roll23   **From** E.Whittlesey,Asst.Comm.NC
Re: *Treatment complaint. (8 pages total)*
STOCKWELL, REV. G.S.   1866/03/07   VA Richmond
Sht 161   S 126 N Roll4   **From** REV. G.S. STOCKWELL
Re: *Seeks employment of colored people.*
STOKES, CHESTER   1866/04/21   VA Richmond
Sht 309   V 255 Y Roll30   **From** Garrick Mallory, Insp., VA
Re: *Unfair hearing by civil magistrate.*
STRAN, WILLIAM   1865/12/22   SC Charleston
Sht 176   S 125 Y Roll24   **From** C.C. Bower, Attorney
Re: *Plaintiff: Recover 2 mules - Mules to be returned.*

STROTHER, DAVID   1865/12/06   MS Yazoo Co.
Sht 371   M 105 Y Roll22   **From** Stuart Eldridge,AAC
Re: *Affidavit concerning "disturbed" state of Co..*

STUART, EARLINE   1866/04/17   VA Staunton   DC Washngtn
Sht 271   J 35 Y Roll28   **From** Augusta Jordan
Re: *Wants to join her husband, JAMES STUART.*

STUART, JAMES   1866/04/17   VA Staunton   DC Washngtn
Sht 271   J 35 Y Roll28   **From** Augusta Jordan
Re: *Being sought by wife, EARLINE STUART.*

SUMMERVAL, JOSEPH   1865/10/07   MD Pt Lookout   MD St. Inigoes
Sht 178   G 3 N Roll3   **From** H.E. Gardner, Asst. QM
Re: *Shot and beaton at St. Inigoes.*

TATNEL, ANSIL   1866/03/13   GA Svannah
Sht 165   S 134 Y Roll29   **From** R. Scott, Brig. General
Re: *Deceased soldier; service back-pay for family.*

TAYLOR, ALLEN   1865/10/16   VA Petersburg   MS Carroll Co.
Sht 267   V 25 N Roll3   **From** O.Brown, Asst.Comm. VA
Re: *Transportation with 7 children to Mississippi.*

TAYLOR, EMMA   1866/04/17   NY New York
Sht 249   H 89 N Roll4   **From** James Harrison
Re: *+Ran away from bondage; owner desires release of obligation.*

TAYLOR, JOHN   1866/03/20   KY Fayette Co.   TN Nashville
Sht 65   B 109 Y Roll26   **From** P. Bonsteel
Re: *Presents case of mistreatment/theft by white person. (K-97)*

TAYLOR, VIRGINIA   1866/01/02   VA Prince Geo.Co.
Sht 293   V 2 Y Roll25   **From** O.Brown, Asst.Comm. VA
Re: *Brutally whipped.*

TEA, ALFRED JOHN   1865/12/06   MS Grenada
Sht 371   M 104 Y Roll22   **From** Stuart Eldridge,AAC
Re: *Complaints of cruelty by employer.*

TEARNOH, GEORGE   1865/09/15   VA Norfolk
Sht 475   T 88 Y Roll18   **From** GEORGE TEARNOH
Re: *Pay for colored laborers Norfolk Navy Yard (Also T-39, T-61)*

THATCHER, GEORGE A. 1865/10/12   VA Leesburg
Sht 203   T 8 N Roll3   **From** GEORGE A. THATCHER
Re: *Superintendent, Colored School/Baptist Church.*

THOMAS, HARLEY   1866/03/19   FL Tallahassee
Sht 241   H 64 Y Roll27   **From** HARLEY THOMAS
Re: *Appeals for justice against rebels.*

THOMAS, REV. J.V.R.   1865/10/04   VA Portsmouth
Sht 202   T 3 N Roll3   **From** REV. J.V.R. THOMAS
Re: *Pastor, Colored Methodist Church.*

THOMAS, WILLIAM   1866/01/06   NC Wilmington
Sht 381   M 11 N Roll3   **From** JOHN MC RAE
Re: *Age 8-10; being sought by JOHN MC RAE.*
THORNTON, A. L.   1866/05/25   VA Richmond
Sht 365   V 319 Y Roll30   **From** O.Brown, Asst.Comm. VA
Re: *Presents resolution to retain present superintendent of VA.*
TOLIVER, JOHN   1866/05/05   WV Culpepper
Sht 111   C 160 N Roll4   **From** W.K. Chase, Asst. Supt.
Re: *Husband of REBECCA TOLIVER, living with Mr. A. Green.*
TOLIVER, REBECCA   1866/05/05   WV Culpepper
Sht 111   C 160 N Roll4   **From** W.K. Chase, Asst. Supt.
Re: *Requests financial assistance from husband, JOHN TOLIVER.*
TOMPKINS, WILLIAM   1865/10/16   DC Washngtn   VA Fairfax Co.
Sht 48   B 12 N Roll3   **From** F.B. Brown, Jail Warden
Re: *Accused of stealing cow, with CHAMP CONNOR.*
TROTTMAN, MAJOR   1866/02/05   NC Roanoke Island
Sht 350   W 36 Y Roll25   **From** THOMAS WHITNEY et al
Re: *Petition: Ration tickets taken away.*
TUBBS, DEMPSEY   1866/02/05   NC Roanoke Island
Sht 350   W 36 Y Roll25   **From** THOMAS WHITNEY et al
Re: *Petition: Ration tickets taken away.*
TUCKER, LAURA   1866/05/19   PA Williamsport
Sht 275   J 42 N Roll4   **From** D. Jamison, Owner
Re: *Bound to owner who no longer wants her.*
TURNER, BENJAMIN   1866/05/14   MS Vicksburg
Sht 383   M 211 N Roll4   **From** T.J. Wood, Major General
Re: *49th USCT, deceased son of KATE PERKINS.*
TURNER, BOATSWAIN   1865/10/27   MS Vicksburg
Sht 100   D 6 Y Roll20   **From** Joe E. Davis
Re: *Former servant at Davis' Bend.*
TURNER, CHARLES   1866/03/27   MD Howard Co.
Sht 99   C 124 Y Roll26   **From** C.H.Howard,Asst.Comm.DC
Re: *Son of CHARLOTTE TURNER.*
TURNER, CHARLOTTE   1866/03/27   MD Howard Co.
Sht 99   C 124 Y Roll26   **From** C.H.Howard,Asst.Comm.DC
Re: *Two children, FRANK and CHARLES, held illegally.*
TURNER, FRANK   1866/03/27   MD Howard Co.
Sht 99   C 124 Y Roll26   **From** C.H.Howard,Asst.Comm.DC
Re: *Son of CHARLOTTE TURNER.*
TURNER, MATTHEW   1865/08/11   MD A. Arundel Co.
Sht 88   D 6 Y Roll14   **From** William Daniel, lawyer
Re: *Reported burning of Magothy Colored M.E. Church.*

TURNER, REV. H. M.   1865/10/24   GA Atlanta
Sht 214   T 63 N Roll3   **From** REV. H.M. TURNER
Re: *Requests transportation to preach to colored.*
TYLER, ELIZA   1865/06/22   MD Baltimore   MS Waverly
Sht 475   T 85 Y Roll18   **From** LIZZIE (ELIZA) TYLER
Re: +*Transportation for children from Mississippi.*
TYLER, THOMAS   1866/03/16   VA Richmond
Sht 277   V 164 N Roll4   **From** O.Brown, Asst.Comm. VA
Re: *Co. H, 1st USCC; receipt for discharge papers.*
TYNES, JAMES   1865/05/27   VA Norfolk
Sht 44   B 95 Y Roll13   **From** JOHN H. BROWN, petitioner
Re: *Missionery for the Freedmen*
UANDALE, MARTIN   1865/09/15   VA Clarksburg
Sht 69   C 61 Y Roll14   **From** A.B. Eaton, Subsist. Comm.
Re: *45th USCT: Rations for wife and family (letter B-89)*
UNCLE, JANE   1866/03/15   DC Washngtn
Sht 91   C 99 N Roll4   **From** C.H. Howard, Brig. General
Re: *Mother to HANNAH WARFIELD (See letter, M-158, March 28).*
UPTON, POLLY   1865/09/20   NY Ellington
Sht 53   B 160 Y Roll13   **From** James Boyden
Re: *Aunt to JULIA MOORE.*
VIRTUE, EDWARD   1866/02/21   GA Augusta   PA Philadelphia
Sht 239   H 36 N Roll3   **From** Albert Hopkins
Re: *Transportation for EDWARD VIRTUE 3 orphans to Philadelphia.*
WADDY, HANNAH   1866/05/23   VA Rappahannock
Sht 205   S 264 N Roll4   **From** R.M. Sanford
Re: *Being sought by husband LOUIS WADDY.*
WADDY, LOUIS   1866/05/23   VA Rappahannock
Sht 205   S 264 N Roll4   **From** R.M. Sanford
Re: *Looking for wife HANNAH WADDY and 6 children.*
WALKER, HENRY   1866/04/16   NY Oneida Co.   DC Washngtn
Sht 295   K 104 N Roll4   **From** F. Koomes
Re: *Seeking back pay as servant. (Also N-104)*
WALKER, JANE   1866/01/15   VA Augusta Co.
Sht 298   V 28 Y Roll25   **From** O.Brown, Asst.Comm. VA
Re: *Beaten by man she lived with.*
WALLACE, JAMES   1866/02/14   GA Svannah
Sht 352   W 46 Y Roll25   **From** ABRAHAM WINFIELD et al
Re: *Petition against miscellaneous "evils." (Also B-2, 1866)*
WALLFORD, JOHN   1865/11/06   MD Baltimore
Sht 84   C 28 N Roll3   **From** J.P. Creagen
Re: *Complains of conditions.*

WARD, LEWIS 1866/04/12 PA Gettysburg WV Westmorlnd
Sht 329 L 71 N Roll4 **From** Q.H. Lott
Re: *Seeking information regarding wife and family.*

WARFIELD, HANNAH 1866/03/28 MD Annapolis
Sht 367 M 158 Y Roll28 **From** Thomas Swann, Governor, MD
Re: *+In penitentiary for assault on former mistress. (See C-91)*

WARNER, HENRY 1866/02/09 PA Philadelphia MD Kent Co.
Sht 108 D 21 Y Roll20 **From** Henry M. Dickert, Atty
Re: *+Nephew of WILLIAM H. HACKETT.*

WARREN, DANIEL 1865/09/16 VA Warrenton VA Alexandria
Sht 237 K 11 N Roll2 **From** F.W. Kingston, Attorney
Re: *Barber, seeking brothers and sisters.*

WASHNGTN, GEORGE 1866/02/28 VA Richmond
Sht 316 V 117 N Roll3 **From** O.Brown, Asst.Comm. VA
Re: *Discharged seaman seeking bounty due.*

WASHNGTN, LUCINDA 1865/09/25 AR Batesville MO St. Louis
Sht 43 B 90 N Roll2 **From** J.T. Bradley
Re: *Seeks pay for services, Batesville Hospital.*

WATKINS, CHARLES A. 1866/03/15 MD Centerville
Sht 335 W 76 Y Roll30 **From** CHARLES A. WATKINS
Re: *Reports outrages on returning Colored soldiers.*

WATSON, MARY 1865/06/30 OH Cincinnati LA New Orleans
Sht 59 C 12 N Roll2 **From** S.T. Chase, Judge
Re: *Imprisoned; unable to collect wages due.*

WATSON, WILLIAM 1865/10/27 MS Vicksburg
Sht 100 D 6 Y Roll20 **From** Joe E. Davis
Re: *Former servant at Davis' Bend.*

WATSON, WILLIAM 1865/10/27 MS Vicksburg
Sht 100 D 6 Y Roll20 **From** Joe E. Davis
Re: *Former servant at Davis' Bend.*

WATTS, WARREN 1865/10/27 MS Vicksburg
Sht 100 D 6 Y Roll20 **From** Joe E. Davis
Re: *Former servant at Davis' Bend.*

WEBSTER, JAMES 1865/09/16 VA Alexandria VA Warrenton
Sht 237 K 11 N Roll2 **From** F.W. Kingston, Attorney
Re: *Seeking brothers and sisters.*

WELTON, JOHN 1866/02/16 VA Hardy Co. MA Boston
Sht 237 H 29 Y Roll21 **From** L.W. Hasking, Navy Dept.
Re: *+Wife, 5 children still with former owner.*

WHITE, GARLAND H. 1866/02/06 GA Svannah
Sht 192 S 80 Y Roll24 **From** Charles Sumner, U.S.Sen.
Re: *Former Chaplain, 28th USCT. (Also W-28, 1866)*

WHITE, GUILFORD 1866/01/06 VA Lynchburg VA Richmond
Sht 295 V 10 N Roll3 **From** O.Brown, Asst.Comm. VA
Re: *Pvt, 13th USCT, died at Freedmen's Hospital, Lynchburg.*
WHITNEY, MC LEAN 1865/10/04 MA Boston NC Cape Fear
Sht 66 P 1 N Roll3 **From** R.M.Price, Insp. Gen.,MA
Re: +*Whitney children being sought by McLean Whitney's employer.*
WHITNEY, THOMAS 1866/02/05 NC Roanoke Island
Sht 350 W 36 Y Roll25 **From** THOMAS WHITNEY et al
Re: *Petition: Ration tickets taken away.*
WICKS, STEPHEN 1865/08/05 VA Norfolk
Sht 63 C 34 Y Roll14 **From** Mayor Daniel Collins
Re: *Arrested, fined for keeping horse and wagon with no license.*
WILLIAMS, ABRAM 1866/04/30 ND Goldsboro
Sht 257 H 117 Y Roll27 **From** Dan T. Horrell, Farm Owner
Re: *Released from jail to work on farm.*
WILLIAMS, FANNIE 1865/09/28 VA Alexandria
Sht 223 H 23 N Roll3 **From** P.H. Hambrick, Prov. Judge
Re: *Breach of promise - ROBERT HOPKINS.*
WILLIAMS, ISAAC 1866/04/26 VA Warrenton DC Washngtn
Sht 77 P 86 Y Roll29 **From** R. Morrow, Asst. AG
Re: *Ill treatment by Bureau agent.*
WILLIAMS, JAMES 1866/05/15 MD Baltimore
Sht 199 S 245 N Roll4 **From** George J.Steward, Supt.,MD
Re: *Seeking moneys owed.*
WILSEY, MARY JANE 1866/05/08 KY Greenburg
Sht 323 V 292 N Roll4 **From** O.Brown, Asst.Comm. VA
Re: *Seeking parents (Scott.)*
WILSON, BENJAMIN 1865/12/14 SC Beaufort
Sht 172 S 110 Y Roll24 **From** C.J. Stallbraith, Brig. Gen.
Re: *Bought mansion; threatened by returned owner.*
WILSON, D. J. 1866/01/27 SC Georgetown
Sht 187 S 54 Y Roll24 **From** I.H. SHECKELFOD
Re: *Petition: Unwilling to sign work contract.*
WILSON, MARTHA 1866/01/25 VA Palmyria
Sht 132 C 28 N Roll3 **From** Montilla Clark, Freedmn Crt
Re: *Certificate of marriage to white soldier, John Anderson.*
WILSON, R. D. 1866/01/27 SC Georgetown
Sht 187 S 54 Y Roll24 **From** I.H. SHECKELFOD
Re: *Petition: Unwilling to sign work contract.*
WINFIELD, ABRAHAM 1866/02/14 GA Svannah
Sht 352 W 46 Y Roll25 **From** ABRAHAM WINFIELD et al
Re: *Petition against miscellaneous "evils." (A. Bradley, lawyer)*

WINSTON, THOMAS   1866/04/06   DC Washngtn
Sht 25   A 184 N Roll4   **From** A.F. Rocknell, Asst. AG
Re: *Private; claims $300 lost by his Lieutenant.*
WITHERS, CHARLEY   1866/04/26   VA Warrenton DC Washngtn
Sht 77   P 86 Y Roll29   **From** R. Morrow, Asst. AG
Re: *Ill treatment by Bureau agent.*
WOOD, CLARISA   1865/07/24   NC New Bern NC Roanoke Isl
Sht 437   S 164 Y Roll17   **From** G.M. Stuart
Re: *Daughter of JOSEPH and REBECCA WOOD (Also W-31).*
WOOD, JENNY   1865/07/24   NC New Bern NC Roanoke Isl
Sht 437   S 164 Y Roll17   **From** G.M. Stuart
Re: *Daughter of JOSEPH and REBECCA WOOD (Also W-31)*
WOOD, JOHNSON   1866/03/24   VA Richmond
Sht 283   V 184 N Roll4   **From** O.Brown, Asst.Comm. VA
Re: *Back pay from Quartermaster Department*
WOOD, JOSEPH   1865/07/24   NC New Bern NC Roanoke Isl
Sht 437   S 164 Y Roll17   **From** G.M. Stuart, former employer
Re: *+Sought by family in Springfield, Mass.*
WOOD, M.   1865/08/11   MD Baltimore DC Washngtn
Sht 8   A 44 N Roll2   **From** C.W. Foster, Asst. Adj Gen
Re: *30th USCT, seeking bounty.*
WOOD, MANNIE   1865/07/24   NC New Bern NC Roanoke Isl
Sht 437   S 164 Y Roll17   **From** G.M. Stuart
Re: *Daughter of JOSEPH and REBECCA WOOD (Also W-31)*
WOOD, REBECCA   1865/07/24   NC New Bern NC Roanoke Isl
Sht 437   S 164 Y Roll17   **From** G.M. Stuart
Re: *Wife of JOSEPH WOOD (Also W-31)*
WOOD, THOMAS   1865/07/24   NC New Bern NC Roanoke Isl
Sht 437   S 164 Y Roll17   **From** G.M. Stuart
Re: *Son of JOSEPH and REBECCA WOOD (Also W-31)*
WRIGHT, RAPHAEL   1865/12/12   VA Richmond
Sht 286   V 127 Y Roll25   **From** O.Brown, Asst.Comm. VA
Re: *Bounter voucher approved.*
YOUNG, CHARLES I.   1866/01/26   MD St. Inigoes
Sht 220   T 28 N Roll3   **From** D. W. Tyler
Re: *Deceased soldier; bounded requested for dependent mother.*
YOUNG, ELLEN   1866/04/19   VA Middlesex
Sht 381   Y 2 N Roll4   **From** ELLEN YOUNG
Re: *Seeking her property left during the war.*

INDEX TWO

**AFRICAN AMERICANS IDENTIFIED IN INDIVIDUAL
REPORTS, PETITIONS, MEETINGS, AND AFFIDAVITS IN
WHICH 24 OR MORE NAMES WERE INCLUDED**

A <u>DESCRIPTIVE LIST</u> of the sources for the names in this index precedes the index of names. The number (**No.**) in the third column of the index corresponds with the Group Number on the <u>DESCRIPTIVE LIST</u>. Column 4 gives the location of the individual, if it is other than what was shown in the correspondence. The abbreviation "CN" represents the Choctaw Nation.

INDEX TWO - African Americans Identified in Reports, Petitions, Affidavits.....

LAST NAME`	FIRST NAME	No	LOCATION
ABRAMS	FRANK	4	
ADAMS	PETER	2	
ADDISON	GEORGE	8	
ADMEYER	JASON	3	
ALDREDGE	JOHN	11	
ALEXANDER	EDWARD	9	Kenton Co. KY
ALEXANDER	HENRY	11	
ALEXANDER	RUEBEN	11	
ALEXANDER	WILLIAM	4	
ALLEN	CORNELIUS	6	Hampton VA
ALLEN	MINOR	9	Bath Co. KY
ALLEN	WILLIAM	8	
ALSTON	ARNOLD	11	
ALSTON	HARRIET	11	
AMBLER	EDWARD	6	Culpepper VA
ANDERSON	CHARLES W.	11	
ANDERSON	DANIEL	3	
ANDERSON	ELI	11	
ANDERSON	LOUIS	2	
ANDERSON	N. H.	6	Richmond VA
ANDREWS	JAMES D.	4	
ARMSTEAD	JOHN	3	
ARTIST	SHEPPARD	11	
ASH	PETER	4	
ASHLEY	P. S.	10	
ATKINS	REUBEN	9	Jessamine Co. KY
AUSTIN	DANIEL	11	
AUSTIN	MARY	11	
BAILEY	AFRICA	11	
BAILEY	ROBERT	6	Hampton VA
BAKER	FREDERICK	3	
BAKER	T.L.R.	6	Norfolk VA
BALL	CUMMINGS	4	
BALL	JOHN	4	
BALL	RICHARD	10	
BALLARD	BENJAMIN	11	
BANES*	ABRAM	10	
BARBER	NICHOLAS	6	Norfolk VA
BARKSDALE	HENRY	6	Danville VA
BARNES*	JEFFERSON	10	
BARNETT	HENRY	3	
BARRON	I. M.	4	
BATES	ISAAC	1	

BATES	JANE	1	
BEACON	LARRY	3	
BEARD	JONAS	11	
BECK	MAJOR	11	
BECKLEY	R. D.	6	Alexandria VA
BELEMY*	BARNEY	10	
BELEY*	EDWARD	10	
BELL	ASAR	3	
BENNETT	JOE	7	
BENNETT	LEWIS	11	
BENNETT	REUBEN	11	
BENNETT	ROMEO	7	
BENSON	JOHN H.	8	
BENTLY	ROBERT	2	
BENTON	CHARLES	4	
BENTON	HENRY	4	
BERRY	FRANK D.	11	
BERRY	THOMAS	8	
BEST	JESSE	9	Grant Co. KY
BIRCH	BRAM	4	
BISHOP	AMANDA	9	Kenton Co. KY
BISHOP	HENRY	9	Kenton Co. KY
BISHOP	SIDNEY	9	Kenton Co. KY
BLACK	MARY	11	
BLACK	PETER	7	
BLACK	THOMPSON	3	
BLAND	THOMAS	3	
BLANTON	GILBERT	3	
BLOOM	PETER	11	
BLOOM	REBECCA AN	11	
BOGGS	SIMON	7	
BOIGIN	DAVID	10	
BOLDER	THOMAS	9	Fayette Co. KY
BOND	HENRY	11	
BOONDWATERS	THOMAS M.	3	
BOONE	THOMAS	11	
BOOTMAN	ANNUAL	3	
BOULAS	THOMMAS	4	
BOWLES	AMOS	11	
BOYENTON*	ALVIN	10	
BOYER	GEORGE	3	
BOYER	WILLIAM	3	
BOYLE	ELIZA	11	
BOYLE	LEWIS	11	
BOYLE	ROBERT	11	

BRADFORD	ALBERT	3	
BRADLEY	WILLIAM	10	
BRADLEY*	FRED	10	
BRANDENED	S.	11	
BRAY	ELISHA	3	
BRIANT	DAVID	10	
BRICE	ISAM	10	
BRIGGS	ARCHIE	3	
BRIGHTMAN	ANDREW	7	
BRISTOL	EDWIN	11	
BROOKS	EDMOND	6	Fredericksburg VA
BROOKS	EDWARD	3	
BROOKS	JAMES	6	Fredericksburg VA
BROOKS	SAM	11	
BROWN	ALEX	8	
BROWN	DOLBERT	4	
BROWN	EDWARD	10	
BROWN	ELLEN	11	
BROWN	HARRIET	5	Jacksfork Co. CN
BROWN	JESSE	10	
BROWN	JOHN H.	8	
BROWN	PETER	4	
BROWN	PETER	11	
BROWN	REV. JOHN M.	6	Norfolk VA
BROWN	ROBERT	3	
BROWN	ROBERT H.	10	
BROWN	SANDY	4	
BROWN	WATSON	5	CN
BROWN	WILLIAM	4	
BROWN	WINNY	5	Jacksfork Co. CN
BROWN	WINSTON	2	
BULTON	E.	3	
BURDETTE	CLARISSA	9	Garrard Co. KY
BURDETTE	ELIJAH	9	Garrard Co. KY
BURKE	JAMES	3	
BURNAM	MANCH	9	Madison Co. KY
BURNET	BUCK	10	
BURNS	PATE	9	Bath Co. KY
BURTON	ROBERT	10	
BUSHEYHEAD	BUCK	5	CN
BUSHEYHEAD	JOSEPHINE	5	Blue County CN
BUSHEYHEAD	LUCYANN	5	Blue County CN
BUSHEYHEAD	MARGARET	5	Blue County CN
BUSHEYHEAD	NANCY	5	Blue County CN
BUSHEYHEAD	NARCISS	5	Blue County CN

BYRNE	DR. THOMAS	6	Norfolk VA
CACHEON	N. W.	3	
CALDWELL	JOSEPH	11	
CALLTE*	EADMUND	4	
CALM	DAVID	6	Petersburg VA
CALVERT*	WILLIAM W.	10	
CAMMIL	QUASH	4	
CAMPBELL	CORY	11	
CAMPBELL	ROBERT	3	
CANODY	SIMMONS	4	
CAPMAN	JAMES	4	
CAR	JACK	10	
CAREY	REV. JOHN	6	Yorktown VA
CARMACK*	ARCHIBALD	8	
CARR	NEWMAN/NORMAN	8	
CARRINGTON	EDWARD	6	Lynchburg VA
CARRUTHERS	DAN	11	
CARTER	LEWIS	6	Petersburg VA
CARTMAN	ADELINE	11	
CARTWRIGHT	RUGG	11	
CASE	GABRIEL	9	Grant Co. KY
CHAFUS*	WILLIAM B.	4	
CHAMBBELD	WILLIAM	4	
CHERRY	ELI	11	
CHERRY	HENRY	10	
CHESTER	G.	11	
CHINN	CHARLES	6	Alexandria VA
CHISLIN	JOSEPH	8	
CHRISTOPHER	HANDY	11	
CLAGGETT	WILLIAM	6	Alexandria VA
CLARK	BEVERLY	2	
COLBERT	BEN	5	CN
COLBERT	JULY	5	Kinnish Co. CN
COLBERT	LUCY	5	Chickasaw Co. CN
COLBERT	MOBEAL	5	Kinnish Co. CN
COLBERT	NANCY	5	Kinnish Co. CN
COLBERT	RACHAEL	5	Kinnish Co. CN
COLE	HENRIETTA	11	
COLE	HENRY	11	
COLE	JOHN	8	
COLEMAN	HANNAH	3	
COLENS	PASS	10	
COLLINS	MILES	9	Boone Co. KY
COLLINS	RICH	8	
COLMINT	C. DENT	10	

CONNACK	NIVERT	10	
COOK	FIELDS	6	Richmond VA
COOK	GEORGE W.	6	Norfolk VA
COOPER	EASTER	11	
CORPREW	GEORGE	6	Norfolk VA
COSBY	ALEXANDER	2	
COTES	COLEMAN	6	Lynchburg VA
COTTON	BEN	11	
COWING	W. J.	6	Alexandria VA
CROMWELL	RICHARD	11	
CROSS	P. A.	6	Charlottesville VA
CRUIZE	ROBERT	3	
CRUSE	GEORGE	11	
CRUTCHFIELD	HENRY	9	Boyle Co. KY
DALLAS	JERRY	7	
DANIEL	DUDLEY	3	
DANIELS	GEORGE	1	
DART	J. F.	4	
DASE*	WILAM	4	
DAVENPORT	DANIEL	3	
DAVIS	BENJAMIN	3	
DAVIS	JOE	11	
DAVIS	JOSEPH	8	
DAVIS	LAMON	11	
DAVIS	MOLLIE	11	
DAVIS	REV. WILLIAM	6	Norfolk VA
DAVIS*	HARRY	10	
DAVISON	HARRY	7	
DEPREE	JANE	11	
DESVERNEYS	JOHN C.	4	
DICKSON	REV. G. L.	6	VA
DIGNON	UMFRY	4	
DIXON	T. E.	4	
DOBSON	F.	11	
DODSON	MANUEL	2	
DOLMAN	GEORGE	1	
DOLMAN	LOUISA	1	
DOLMAN	LUCINDA	1	
DOLMAN	MOSES	1	
DONNELOIB*	SAM	10	
DORSEY	CORA	9	Fayette Co. KY
DORSEY	JOHN H.	8	
DOUGLAS	J. P.	6	Alexandria VA
DOULAS	SHAMMUS	4	
DOVE	OWEN	10	

DREW	CORNELIUS	8	
DUNLAP	GEORGE	11	
DUNLOP	A.	6	Hampton VA
DUPREE	MARY	11	
DURDEN	ELDRIEGE	1	
DURDEN	HANNAH	1	
DURDEN	JOHN	1	
DURDEN	PETER	1	
DURDEN	ROSA	1	
EDMONDS	MOSES	3	
EDWARDS	B. T.	6	Manchester VA
EDWARDS	JOE	7	
EVANS	CATHERINE	11	
EVANS	EDWARD/EDMUND	11	
EVENS	WILLIAM	2	
FARRALL	HENRY	9	Nicholas Co. KY
FELL	ALBERT	4	
FERREE	CAPTAIN	6	Alexandria VA
FINLEY	BOSTON	4	
FINLEY	CHARLES	4	
FINLEY	JOROCH	4	
FINLEY	MOSES	4	
FINLEY*	EXICEOR	4	
FINLEY*	VATRUM	4	
FINNEY	JORDAN	9	Boone Co. KY
FISHER	ALEXANDER	5	Choctaw Co. CN
FISHER	ELENA	5	Choctaw Co. CN
FISHER	FRANCIS	5	Choctaw Co. CN
FISHER	ISABELLA	5	Choctaw Co. CN
FISHER	IVERSON	5	Choctaw Co. CN
FISHER	JOHNEY	5	Choctaw Co. CN
FISHER	MARIAH	5	Choctaw Co. CN
FISHER	MERITY	5	Choctaw Co. CN
FISHER	ORLY	5	Choctaw Co. CN
FISHER	PANCHUNA	5	Choctaw Co. CN
FISHER	TRENSAL	5	Choctaw Co. CN
FISHER	WILLIAM	5	Choctaw Co. CN
FLETCHER	JANE	11	
FLUD	ADAM	4	
FOLKS	JOSEPH	2	
FORD	RICHARD	8	
FORD	WASHINGTON	3	
FORD	WILLIAM W.	6	Fairfax VA
FORST	JOHN	10	
FOSTER	STEPHEN	3	

FOWLER	ARMSTEAD	9	Fayette Co. KY
FOWNED	HARRY	11	
FRANCIS	JOHN	3	
FRANCIS	WILLIAM H.	8	
FRANKLIN	GEORGE	6	Alexandria VA
FRASER	I. A.	4	
FRASHER	JAMES	4	
FRASUR	SAMSON	4	
FREMAN	A.	10	
FRISBY	GEORGE H.	8	
FRISBY	JOHN	8	
FROME	JOEL	9	Madison Co. KY
FULLER	MINGO	4	
GADSON	JOHN	4	
GAILLARD	PAUL	7	
GAINES	HENRY	9	Kenton Co. KY
GAINES	MARY	9	Kenton Co. KY
GANS	TOMMAS	10	
GARDNER	JANE	5	Danksville Co. CN
GARDNER	JOHN	5	Danksville Co. CN
GARDNER	LAURY	5	Danksville Co. CN
GARDNER	NISSA	5	Danksville Co. CN
GARDNER	RANDOLPH	5	CN
GARDNER	TENNESSEE	5	Danksville Co. CN
GARNESS*	H.	10	
GARNETT	REV. HIGHLAND H.	6	Washington DC
GASTNER	R.	10	
GATLIN	CHARLES	10	
GIBBS	F. G.	10	
GIBBS	FRED	10	
GIBBS	THOMAS	10	
GILLIAN	LAUZEE	11	
GILMORE*	THOMAS	10	
GIPSON	ISAAC	11	
GLA	I. A.	3	
GLASGOW	SCOTT	3	
GLUVER	THOMMUS	4	
GOCY	GARRISON	3	
GODDEL	JACKSON	11	
GODDEL	LAURA	11	
GOING	PRINCE	3	
GOODALL	MARSHALL	2	
GOODLAW	JANE	11	
GORDON	NATHANIEL	3	
GRADY	MARY	11	

GRAHAM	RICHARD	4	
GRANT	ABRAHAM	4	
GRANT	CYRUS	7	
GRANT	D.	4	
GRANT	GEORGE	4	
GRANT	TOM	4	
GRAVES	WILLIAM	8	
GRAY	ABNER	3	
GREEN	ANTENNY	4	
GREEN	CHARLES	4	
GREEN	GEORGE	3	
GREEN	GRANVILLE	3	
GREEN	JOSHUA	10	
GREEN	MARTHA	9	Fayette Co. KY
GREEN	WILLIAM	10	
GREEN	WILLIAM	11	
GRIER	ELIZA	11	
GRIFFIN	HENRY	2	
GRIGGS	DAVID	9	Boone Co. KY
GRIGGS	GABRIEL	9	Boone Co. KY
GRIGGS	HARRISON	9	Kenton Co. KY
GRIGGS	LEVINA	9	Boone Co. KY
GRIGGS	PHILIP	9	Boone Co. KY
GROGAN*	MINGO	4	
GROVES	ALFRED	3	
GUCHE*	SGT. CHARLES	10	
HALL	CORNELIA	11	
HALL	SOLOMON	11	
HALLAN	TASH	10	
HAMILTON	KIT	10	
HAMILTON	WILLIAM	3	
HANDY	ALEX	8	
HANDY	JOHN	11	
HANSON	JACOB	8	
HARDY	JOHN	3	
HARRIS	ALBERT	11	
HARRIS	CHARLES	11	
HARRISON	BUCK	5	Kinnish Co. CN
HARRISON	DINAH	5	Kinnish Co. CN
HARRISON	MAZE	11	
HARRISON	NANCY	5	Kinnish Co. CN
HARRISON	SARY	5	Kinnish Co. CN
HARRISON	VISAL	5	Kinnish Co. CN
HAWKINS	DAVID	11	
HAWKINS	SALLIE	11	

HAYWOOD	J.	10	
HENDERSON	DAVID	3	
HENDERSON	THOMAS H.	10	
HENSON	REV. THOMAS	6	Norfolk VA
HERSEY	HANNAH	11	
HILL	NATHANIEL	4	
HILL	RICHARD	6	Williamsburg VA
HILL	SAMUEL	10	
HILL*	IDA	10	
HILL*	VIRGIL	10	
HILLERY	SAMUEL	3	
HIND	WILLIAM	10	
HINES	DANIEL	10	
HINES	JAMES	2	
HOBSON	R. C.	6	Richmond VA
HODGES	REV. WILLIAM J.	6	Norfolk VA
HOLMAN	WILLIAM	6	Fairfax VA
HOLMES	DUNCAN	10	
HOLMES	MASON	10	
HOOD	WYLIE	3	
HOOPER	JOSEPH	8	
HOPSOME	CAREY	6	Hampton VA
HORTLY	BILLY	7	
HOWARD	GEORGE	11	
HOWARD	WESLEY	8	
HOWELL*	DAVID	10	
HOWLET	CHARLEY	11	
HUBBARD	LEROY T.	10	
HUGHES	ISAAC	3	
HUGHES	PETER	9	Nicholas Co. KY
HUMES	SAMUEL	4	
HUMPHREY	MORRIS	11	
HUNT	HENRY	11	
HUNT	LUCY	11	
HUNT	SALLY	9	Fayette Co. KY
HUSTON	JAMES	3	
INGRAHAM	ELIZA	11	
IVES	WILLIAM L.	6	Alexandria VA
JACKMON	J. W.	6	Goucester VA
JACKS*	JACK.	10	
JACKSON	BENJAMIN	6	Danville VA
JACKSON	EDWARD	11	
JACKSON	HENRY	11	
JACKSON	JUNE	4	
JACKSON	PETER	3	

KELLEY	GEORGIANNE	11	
KELLOGG	WILLIAM J.	10	
KEMP	BETTY ADELINE	5	Choctaw Co. CN
KEMP	CALDONA	5	Chickasaw Co. CN
KEMP	CHARLES	5	Chickasaw Co. CN
KEMP	DICKSON	5	Choctaw Co. CN
KEMP	ELIJAH	5	Chickasaw Co. CN
KEMP	ELIZABETH	5	Chickasaw Co. CN
KEMP	FRANCIS	5	Chickasaw Co. CN
KEMP	HARRY	5	Chickasaw Co. CN
KEMP	HENRY	5	CN
KEMP	ISAAC	5	CN
KEMP	JERRY	5	CN
KEMP	JOHN	5	Choctaw Co. CN
KEMP	LEANDER	5	Chickasaw Co. CN
KEMP	MANUEL	5	Choctaw Co. CN
KEMP	MARY	5	Chickasaw Co. CN
KEMP	MOSES	5	Choctaw Co. CN
KEMP	NANCY	5	Choctaw Co. CN
KEMP	SUSAN	5	Chickasaw Co. CN
KERNEY	MARGARET	11	
KERSEY	AUGUST	2	
KILSON	SAMUEL	6	Lynchburg VA
KNIGHT	MOSES	7	
LACEY	EDWIN	11	
LANDRUM	HENRY	3	
LANE	BILL	10	
LANE	EMMA	11	
LANE	JOHN W.	11	
LANG	SARAH	11	
LE MIER	PENNY	11	
LEE	LEWIS	11	
LEE	S. H.	6	Fairfax VA
LEMON	OLD	9	Madison Co. KY
LEWIS	JOHN	11	
LIVELY	WILLIAM	6	Petersburg VA
LOCKE	ADAM	11	
LONG	FANNY	11	
LONG	ROBERT	3	
LONG	SARAH	11	
LONG	SHADE	11	
LOOMAN	DANIEL	5	CN
LOOMAN	ROBERT	5	Kinnish Co. CN
LOOMAN	SOPHA	5	Kinnish Co. CN
LOUIS	OLLIVER	2	

LOUNSE	BARNABE	3	
MAC	HENRY	10	
MAC CAMON	HENRY	10	
MACK	SY	4	
MACK	WILLIAM	4	
MADDIL	JANIEL K.	3	
MAGUIRE*	SILAS	10	
MAKER*	JAMES	10	
MAKINS	EDWARD	10	
MALESBERRY*	A.	10	
MALONE	JOHN	11	
MALONE	SANDY	10	
MALVERN	HENRY	6	Alexandria VA
MARIANO	A. C.	4	
MARSHALL	JULIA	11	
MARTIN	E. H.	10	
MARTIN	WILLIAM H.	10	
MASES*	M. W.	10	
MASON	ELIZA	1	
MASON	JERRY	1	
MASON	MIRANDA	1	
MASON	ROSA	1	
MASON	WILEY	11	
MASON	WILLIAM T.	8	
MATHUSE*	GHANSON	4	
MAXWELL	CHARLES	4	
MAXWELL	PRINCE	7	
MAXWELL	STEPHEN	4	
MC BRIDE*	BRANDEN	10	
MC CALLAM	JASPER	11	
MC CANTS	THOMAS	4	
MC COY	KING	10	
MC GONNAL*	W..	4	
MC LANE	JOHN	10	
MC NEIL	ARCHIE	3	
MENCES*	ESAS	10	
MENSES	JOSH	10	
MERRICK	I. H.	10	
MERRICK	RICHARD	10	
MERRIWEATHER	MARY A.	11	
MICHUM	CALDONIA	11	
MIDDENTON	HENRY	10	
MIDDLETON	ABRAHAM	4	
MIDDLETON	I. B.	4	
MIDDLETON	JAMES	4	

MIDDLETON	THOMAS	4	
MIKELS	FRANK	4	
MILBURN	GEORGE	8	
MILLAR	POMAY	4	
MINOR	JOHN	3	
MITCHELL	JACK	3	
MITCHELL	JAMES	4	
MITCHELL	JAMES	10	
MONDESS*	B. S.	4	
MONROE	ELIJAH	6	Goucester VA
MOON	KELLUM	11	
MOORE	FRISBY	8	
MOORE	SI	10	
MOORE	T. T.	10	
MOORE*	ALEXANDER	10	
MORGAN	ABRAM	7	
MORRIS	SAM	10	
MORRIS*	DAVIS	10	
MOSBEY	EDWARD	2	
MOSELEY	RICHARD	3	
MOSELY	JAMES	6	Norfolk VA
MOSELY	WILLIAM	6	Goochland VA
MOSS	CLAYBORN	11	
MOTON	HARRIET	11	
MOULTRICE*	JOSEPH B.	4	
MURRAY	W. F.	4	
NASH	CAPT. S. W.	10	
NAZARETH	THOMAS	10	
NELSON	PATIENCE	11	
NELSON	WILLIAM	4	
NEMENS*	MORIE	10	
NEWSON	M. T.	3	
NICKERS	TIFFER	10	
NICKERSON	THOMAS	3	
NORRIS	ROBERT	10	
NORTON	D. M.	6	Yown VA
ODUM	ANNA	11	
OLIVER	HAMILTON	3	
OLIVER	HENRY	8	
ONY	JO	4	
OWENS	ALEXANDER	2	
PAGE	RUBEN	2	
PAIGE,, JR.	THOMAS F.	6	Norfolk VA
PALITE*	TAFFY	4	
PARK	PETER	3	

PARKER	MACK	11	
PARKER	REV. GEORGE W.	6	Alexandria VA
PARKER	SAMUEL	3	
PARSON	B. C.	4	
PATEN	RICHARD	10	
PATRICK	SAM	10	
PATTERSON	JOSEPH	11	
PECK	NATHANIEL	8	
PEEPERS	HENRY	11	
PERKINS	FRANCIS	11	
PERKINS	HARRY	11	
PERKINS	ISAAC	11	
PERRY	AGGA	5	Chickasaw Co. CN
PERRY	ANNY	5	Chickasaw Co. CN
PERRY	BECEAL	5	Chickasaw Co. CN
PERRY	CHARLES	5	Chickasaw Co. CN
PERRY	E. J.	4	
PERRY	GEORGE	5	
PERRY	JOHN N.	11	
PERRY	LUCY	5	Chickasaw Co. CN
PERRY	SANDERS	5	Chickasaw Co. CN
PERRY	SIMON	5	Chickasaw Co. CN
PETTYJOHN	DOCTOR	6	Alexandria VA
PEYTON	BENJAMIN	6	Fredericksburg VA
PICKETT	ADELADE	11	
PICKETT	SOLOMON	11	
PIERCE	WILLIAM	3	
PLEASANT	WILLIAM	11	
POLK	COLUMBUS	11	
POPE	B.	10	
POPE	WESLEY	10	
PORTER	HENRY	11	
PORTER	MOSES	11	
POWELL	AMOS	8	
PREMIER	LEMUAL	11	
PREMIER	PHILLIS	11	
PRICE	GEORGE	11	
PRICE	REUBEN	3	
RAILE	JACOB	9	Boone Co. KY
RALLS	JOSEPH	9	Bath Co. KY
RANKIN	JOHN A.	3	
READ	THOMAS	10	
REED	WILLIAM	11	
RICHARDSON	FREDERIC	3	
RICHARDSON	JERRY	7	

RICHARDSON	LONDON	7	
RICHARDSON	STEPHNEY	7	
RICHARDSON	TOBY	7	
RICKMAN	REV. NICHOLAS	6	Charlottesville VA
RILEY	COLUMBUS	11	
RILY*	EDWARD	4	
RINGGOLD	GEORGE	8	
RITTER	E. H.	10	
ROBERTSON	WILLIAM	2	
ROBERTSON	WILLIAM	3	
ROBINSON	GEORGE	11	
ROBINSON	JOHN	11	
ROBINSON	NELSON	11	
ROBINSON	REV. C.	6	Alexandria VA
ROBINSON	SHACK	11	
ROBINSON	THOMAS	11	
ROBSON	SY	4	
RORST	CARTER	9	Grant Co. KY
ROSS	JOSEPH	11	
ROSS	LINS	9	Kenton Co. KY
ROURK	G. P.	10	
RUBBY	JAMES	8	
RUFFIN	ROBERT	6	Yorktown VA
SAMPSON	CHARLES	10	
SAMPSON	WILLIAM	10	
SANDERFORD	JAMES N.	8	
SANDERS	NANCY	11	
SANDERS	WILLIAM N.	11	
SAVAGE	HOUSTON	11	
SAVAGE	JIM	11	
SAVIGES*	SANDY	10	
SAWYER	B.	4	
SAYER	ALBERT	10	
SCOTT	EDWARD	8	
SCOTT	JOSEPH	3	
SCOTT	LEWIS	6	Danville VA
SCOTT	WILLIAM	4	
SHACKLEFORD	WILLIAM	3	
SHEAFF	WILLIAM H.	8	
SHINGLETON	JAMES	4	
SHUT*	ROBARD	4	
SIDNEY	KING	3	
SIMMONS	ANTHONY	11	
SIMMONS	CELIA	11	
SIMMONS	PRINCE	4	

SIMMONS	SAMUEL	10	
SIMMONS	WILLIE	10	
SIMONS	ABRAM W.	4	
SIMPSON	JOHN	4	
SIMS	G. W.	6	Washington DC
SIMSON	CHARLES	10	
SINGLETON	SAM	7	
SLABNE*	DAVID	10	
SLEET	ELIZA	9	Grant Co. KY
SLEET	WILLIAM	9	Grant Co. KY
SMALLS	AUGUST	4	
SMALLS	FRANCIS	4	
SMALLS	JULY	4	
SMALLS	JUNE	4	
SMALLS	PETER	4	
SMITH	AVON	11	
SMITH	BAYLESS	3	
SMITH	CHARITY	9	Estelle Co. KY
SMITH	CHARLES	3	
SMITH	DAVID	9	Estelle Co. KY
SMITH	FREDERICK	6	Williamsburg VA
SMITH	J. T.	4	
SMITH	JOHN	10	
SMITH	REV. JORDAN	6	Manchester VA
SMITH	WILLIAM	2	
SMITH	WILLIAM W.	10	
SNOW	THOMAS	10	
SNOWDEN	WILLIAM	3	
SPARROW	HORACE	9	Fayette Co. KY
SPARROW	JACK	9	Fayette Co. KY
SPEARING	DANIEL	7	
SPEARING	THOMAS	7	
SPOTSWELL	PETER	6	Hampton VA
SPRATLEY	ADELIN	1	
SPRATLEY	BEN	1	
SPRATLEY	MARGARET	1	
SPRATLEY	SARAH	1	
SPRINGS*	DICK	10	
STAVENS	CHARLES	10	
STERNER	DANDRIDGE	3	
STEWARD	JOHN	4	
STEWARD	MARY	1	
STEWART	ELIJAH	8	
STEWART	WILLIAM	10	
STOCKLEY	OBADIAH	11	

STOKES	JOSEPH	8	
STREET	JULY	7	
STRICKLAND	STINER	10	
SULLIVAN	JAMES	10	
SWAN	EDWARD	8	
TALLY	F.	11	
TANDY	LEWIS	9	Fayette Co. KY
TASKER	RICHARD	8	
TAYLOR	APRIL	4	
TAYLOR	BOB	11	
TAYLOR	FAIRFAX	6	Charlottesville VA
TAYLOR	HENRY	8	
TAYLOR	JOHN	9	Madison Co. KY
TEAMOTH	GEORGE	6	Portsmouth VA
TELFAIR	JOSHUA	10	
THOMAS	BARTLEY	11	
THOMAS	HORACE	3	
THOMAS	JOHN	3	
THOMAS	REV. J.R.V.	6	Portsmouth VA
THOMAS	RICHARD	8	
THOMAS	WILLIAM D.	8	
THOMAS*	JOHN	10	
THOMMUS	RICHARDAELUVE	4	
THOMPSON	ALBERT	3	
THOMPSON	ANGELINE	5	Blue County CN
THOMPSON	ELIZABETH	5	Blue County CN
THOMPSON	GRUNDY	5	CN
THOMPSON	HARRISON	5	CN
THOMPSON	HENRY	5	Blue County CN
THOMPSON	JAMES	5	Blue County CN
THOMPSON	JANE	5	Blue County CN
THOMPSON	JOHN	2	
THOMPSON	LOUIS	3	
THOMPSON	MEHALY	5	Blue County CN
THOMPSON	POMPEY	5	Blue County CN
THOMPSON	RACHAEL	5	Blue County CN
THOMPSON	WILLIAM	5	Blue County CN
THOMPSON	WILLSON	5	CN
THORNTON	WILLIAM	6	VA
TIBBS	LUCY	11	
TINSLEY	WASHINGTON	3	
TOLBART	MATHEW	3	
TOLBERT	ANTENNY	4	
TOLES	FRED	11	
TOWNSEND	CYNTHIA	11	

TOWSON	WILLIAM	8	
TRUMBLE	H. F.	6	Norfolk VA
TUCKER	BEN	11	
TUESTER	NATHAN	11	
TURNER	CICERO	3	
TURNER	HENRY	3	
TURNER	JOHNSON	3	
TURNER	NELSON	3	
TURNER	REUBEN	3	
TYLER	SAMUEL	8	
TYRES	REV. JAMES	6	Norfolk VA
UNDERWOOD	JACOB	11	
UNDERWOOD	V.	10	
VANDERFORD	JAMES H.	8	
VAUGHN	WILLIAM	11	
VERNON	EDWARD	10	
VESEY	W. S.	10	
VESY*	HENRY	10	
VICTOR	CYNTHIA	9	Nicholas Co. KY
WALKER	ELVIRA	11	
WALKER	FREDERIC	3	
WALKER	I. S.	6	VA
WALKER	JOHN	11	
WALKER	LIZIE	9	Madison Co. KY
WALKER	MARY	11	
WALKER	REV. WILLIAM E.	6	Petersburg VA
WALLACE	CHARLEY	11	
WALLACE	EDWARD	10	
WALLACE*	ARCHIBALD	10	
WALTON	DEMOS	4	
WARD	AUGAS	4	
WARE	MARTHA	11	
WARE	WESLEY	11	
WASHINGTON	ADDISON	6	Amherst VA
WASHINGTON	GEORGE	3	
WASHINGTON	J. H.	6	Fredericksburg VA
WASHINGTON	JAMES	8	
WASHINGTON	PINE O.	3	
WATERS*	R.	10	
WATKINS	ANDREW CHIEF	5	CN
WATKINS	CHARLES	5	Pushmatah Co. CN
WATKINS	JACOB	5	Pushmatah Co. CN
WATKINS	JAMES	5	Pushmatah Co. CN
WATSON	ALBERT	11	
WATSON	AMOS	4	

WEAVER	WILLIAM	3	
WEBB	ALONZO W.	8	
WESLEY	JOHN	11	
WEST	GEORGE	10	
WEST	JOSHUA	3	
WEST	LOUIS	3	
WHITE	ALBERT	10	
WHITE	DAVID	7	
WHITE	JAMES	3	
WHITE	NATHAN	3	
WHITE	PRIMUS	3	
WHITE	SAMPSON	6	VA
WHITE	SILAS	3	
WHITE	WILLIAM	10	
WHITLEY	HORACE	11	
WHITLEY	NANCY	11	
WHITLEY	WILLIAM	11	
WHITTEN	L. S.	6	VA
WIGGINS	J. B.	6	VA
WILCOX	ROBERT	3	
WILKERSON	JEFF	2	
WILKINS	SOLOMON	3	
WILLARD	PECE	4	
WILLIAMS	ABRAM	3	
WILLIAMS	CHRISTOPHER	3	
WILLIAMS	EDWARD W.	6	Norfolk VA
WILLIAMS	HARRIET	11	
WILLIAMS	JACOB	10	
WILLIAMS	JAMES	10	
WILLIAMS	JERRY	11	
WILLIAMS	WALTER	6	Warwick VA
WILLS	RICHARD	6	Hampton VA
WILSON	DANIEL	3	
WILSON	FELIX	11	
WILSON	JOSEPH THOMAS	6	Norfolk VA
WILSON	JOSHUA	6	Portsmouth VA
WINDHAM	ABNER	3	
WINNOW	ROBERT	10	
WINTER	ANDREW	11	
WIT	CHARLES	4	
WIT	J. W.	4	
WIT	JOHN	4	
WOOD	J.	8	
WOOD	JULIUS	11	
WOODFALL	PLEASANT	11	

APPENDIX A

NATIONAL ARCHIVES AND RECORDS ADMINISTRATION REGIONAL BRANCHES

New England Region
380 Trapelo Road
Waltham, MA 02154
(617) 647-8100

Northeast Region
201 Varick Street
New York, NY 10014
(212) 337-1300

Mid-Atlantic Region
9th & Market St., Room 1350
Philadelphia, PA 19107
(215) 597-3000

Southeast Region
1557 St. Joseph Avenue
East Point, GA 30344
(404) 763-7477

Great Lakes Region
7358 S. Pulaski Road
Chicago, IL 60629
(312) 581-7816

Central Plains Region
2312 E. Bannister Road
Kansas City, MO 64131
(816) 926-6272

Southwest Region
501 W. Felix Street
Ft. Worth, TX 76115
(817) 334-5525

Rocky Mountain Region
Bldg. 48, Denver Federal Ctr
Denver, CO 80225-0307
(303) 236-0817

Pacific Southwest Region
2400 Avila Road
Laguna Niguel, CA 92656
(714) 643-4241

Pacific Sierra Region
1000 Commodore Drive
San Bruno, CA 94066
(415) 876-9009

Pacific Northwest Region
6125 Sand Point Way N.E.
Seattle, WA 98115
(206) 526-6507

Alaska Region
654 W. Third Avenue
Anchorage, AK 99501
(907) 271-2441

APPENDIX B.

FORMER OWNERS OF FREEDMEN NAMED IN LETTERS TO THE HEADQUARTERS, BRFAL, MARCH 1865 THROUGH MAY 1866.

FREED PERSON

Last Name	First Name	FORMER OWNER
ANDREWS	CHARLES	James Sweat, Ware Co., GA
BOND	S.	Yates Barbour
BOWSER	NANCY	S.N. Cadiville, Coinjock Bridge, NC
BOYD	TALL	James Howel, Towns Co., GA
CHILDRESS	MILES	Thomas Woodward
DIXON	AGNES	Martha E. Terrell
DORSEY	JOHN	Thomas Sand / Sanders
EVANS	JERRY	Patrick Henry Aylett, Richmond, VA
FRAZIER	FRANK	Eli Millett
GILES	JAMES	Dr. William Gilliston, SC
GREEN	WASHINGTON	James Quisenbury
GROSE	JOHN	William Baney, Charles Co., MD
HACKETT	WILLIAM H.	Benjamin McGinnis, Kent Co., MD
HALL	JOHN	B.F. Landers, Orange Co., VA
HANDY	MRS. JOHN	Colonel John Walton
HANNAH	HENRY	May Clarke
HARRIS	RUEBEN	Isaac Rucker
HENDERSON	ANN	I.M. Henderson
HENDSON	JANUARY	Thomas W. Conner, Macon, GA
HINSON	FRISBY	W.H. Beck
HUTTEN	HARRIETT	Sextus Hutten, Forestville, VA
JOHNSON	PETER	Thomas Ridley
KELLY	WILLIS	James Sweat, Ware Co., GA
KING	GEORGE	John Scriven
KIRKLAND	CHARLES	William Griffin
LANKFORD	ISASA	George W. Lankford
MERIDITH	ELISHA	(son of) Robert E. Lee
MOORE	JULIA	Mrs. Jones, Rappahannock, VA
MORGAN	JAMES	John C. Morgan, Clinch Co., GA
MORTON	JOHN	Gibson Plantation, Bayou Blue, LA
NEWMAN	FRANKY	Pack Malone
RYALL	FERDINAND	Walter C. Caliver, Franklin Co., VA
SCOTT	DAVID	William Carter, Hanover, VA
SCROGGINS	JANE	Captain Tomson, Aquia Creek, VA
TAYLOR	EMMA	James Harrison
TYLER	ELIZA	John L. Hardin, MA
WARFIELD	HANNAH	Margaret Dorsey
WARNER	HENRY	Benjamin McGinnis, Kent Co., MD
WELTON	JOHN	T.B. Welton, Merrifield, VA
WHITNEY	MC CLEAN	Van Bucklin, Cape Fear River, NC
WOOD	JOSEPH	William Wood, Chowan Co., NC

No.	LAST NAME	FIRST NAME	Age	Wage	Sent to:	St
704	ADAMS	WILLIAM	25	12.00	Helena	AR
323	ADRICK	THOMAS	22	8.00	Millersville	MD
285	AIKINS	CALVIN	30	8.00	Port Tobacco	MD
1063	ALDEN	WILLIAM	21	15.00	Lake Providence	LA
614	ALEXANDER	ANNA	21	3.33	Snickersville	VA
437	ALEXANDER	EUGENE	18	.00	Edgehill	VA
613	ALEXANDER	HENRY	28	10.00	Snickersville	VA
436	ALEXANDER	JAMES	21	.00	Edgehill	VA
972	ALLEN	JOHN	26	15.00	Carolina Landing	MS
1011	ALLEN	MARTIN	21	15.00	Lake Providence	LA
650	ALLEN	MARY E.	19	4.00	Lincoln	VA
540	ANDERSON	ALEXANDER	25	10.00	Canton	MS
1004	ANDERSON	CHARLES	22	15.00	Lake Providence	LA
72	ANDERSON	JOHN	24	.00	Hoods Mill	MD
544	ANDERSON	JOHN	15	6.00	Canton	MS
370	ANDERSON	MARY T.	60	.00	Davidsonville	MD
301	ANDERSON	WILLIAM	16	3.50	Allens Fresh	MD
435	ANSEY	THOMAS	30	.00	Edgehill	VA
192	ARCHER	MOSE	18	9.12	Mansfield	OH
1031	ARCHER	RICHARD	24	15.00	Lake Providence	LA
352	BAILY	AGNES	22	5.00	Charlotte Hall	MD
123	BAILY	HENRY	25	10.00	Millersville	MD
872	BAILY	WILLIAM H.	20	15.00	Carolina Landing	MS
597	BAKER	MICHAEL	23	8.00	Huntingtown	MD
929	BALLARD	AARON	19	15.00	Carolina Landing	MS
926	BALLARD	JOHN	37	15.00	Carolina Landing	MS
293	BANKS	DILSEY	28	.00	Baltimore	MD
295	BANKS	JUDY	8	.00	Baltimore	MD
640	BANKS	LEWIS	30	9.00	Huntingtown	MD
294	BANKS	MARY	10	.00	Baltimore	MD
299	BANKS	MILLIE	24	3.33	Chaptico	MD
292	BANKS	NAT	36	10.00	Baltimore	MD
294	BANKS	NAT	4	.00	Baltimore	MD
1025	BARGE	JOHN	22	15.00	Lake Providence	LA
1048	BARNES	AUSTIN	26	15.00	Lake Providence	LA
598	BARNES	JAMES H.	16	3.00	Huntingtown	MD
1050	BARNES	MARY	18	10.00	Lake Providence	LA
944	BARRY	JAMES	28	15.00	Carolina Landing	MS
165	BARRY	MAJOR	30	10.00	King George	VA
341	BASCOM	JOHN	19	8.33	Baltimore	MD
697	BATTISON	PAUL	24	12.00	Helena	AR
699	BATTISON	PETER	29	12.00	Helena	AR
974	BAXTER	SAMUEL	28	15.00	Carolina Landing	MS
97	BEAUFORD	RICHARD	21	25.00	Acquia Creek Land.	MD
803	BEDFORD	ALMSTED	30	15.00	Carolina Landing	MS
804	BELL	ANN	17	9.00	Carolina Landing	MS
10	BELL	WILLIAM	35	10.00	Bladensburg	MD
648	BENJAMIN	JOHN	27	8.00	Newburg	MD
575	BENSON	GEORGE D.	29	10.00	Canton	MS
245	BERRY	ADELINE	24	9.00	Bladensburg	MD
1021	BERRY	ALFRED	29	15.00	Lake Providence	LA
1119	BERRY	ALFRED	21	.00	Baltimore	MD
426	BERRY	GILDA	24	8.33	Mt. Vernon	IL
246	BERRY	MARY	7	.00	Bladensburg	MD

305	BEVERLY	TEMPLE	24	9.00	West River	MD
683	BILLIP	HIRAM	26	10.00	Hillsboro	VA
989	BINGHAM	GEORGE	26	10.00	Allentown	PA
419	BIRD	LEWIS	28	8.33	Pamunkey	MD
978	BLACK	SAMUEL	30	15.00	Carolina Landing	MS
682	BLAIR	PRESLY	23	10.00	Hillsboro	VA
339	BLAKELEY	JAMES	30	8.33	Baltimore	MD
340	BLAKELEY	MARIA	20	3.33	Baltimore	MD
253	BLAKELEY	MILLIE	20	6.00	Chaptico	MD
322	BLAKELEY	MILLIE	20	4.00	Millersville	MD
252	BLAKELEY	SQUIRE	40	11.00	Chaptico	MD
298	BLAKELEY	SQUIRE	36	8.33	Chaptico	MD
321	BLAKELEY	SQUIRE	26	8.33	Millersville	MD
124	BLAKER	SQUIRE	22	10.00	Millersville	MD
591	BLANCHARD	HAMILTON	36	10.00	Canson	MS
433	BLUSKURLE*	ROBERT	32	.00	Edgehill	VA
1141	BOAR	MARY	18	.00	Philadelphia	PA
612	BOGAN	DICK	34	10.00	Snickersville	VA
1074	BOLDEN	ROBERT	21	.00	Philadelphia	PA
1075	BOLDEN	SARAH	20	.00	Philadelphia	PA
449	BOLER	AVA	32	20.00	Cuyahaga	OH
986	BOND	EVANS	12	1.00	Allentown	PA
163	BONNER*	EDWARD	24	20.00	Waterford	PA
673	BORDIS	WILLIAM	22	8.00	Bladensburg	MD
1014	BOSLIS*	HENRY	27	15.00	Lake Providence	LA
428	BOSS	HENRY	19	10.00	Corwnsville	MD
74	BOSSELE	SAMUEL	24	.00	Hoods Mill	MD
521	BOULDER	MARTHA	36	4.00	Collington	MD
523	BOULDER	MARY	4	.00	Collington	MD
522	BOULDER	NANCY	6	.00	Collington	MD
403	BOURIN*	ALLISON	24	8.33	Millersville	MD
364	BOWLEY	C. C.	13	3.33	Silver Creek	MD
755	BOWLING	GEORGE	19	12.00	Helena	AR
885	BOWMAN	HENRY	27	15.00	Carolina Landing	MS
887	BOWMAN	MARY	22	9.00	Carolina Landing	MS
677	BOWMAN	THOMAS	18	8.00	Arnolds Store	MD
821	BOYER	WILLIAM	17	10.00	Carolina Landing,	MS
394	BRADLY	BENJAMIN	14	3.33	Piscataway	MD
194	BRADLY	JAMES	30	9.17	Aquasco	MD
431	BRAXTON	GEORGE	28	.00	Edgehill	VA
328	BRIGGS	WILLIAM	16	5.00	Millersville	MD
1129	BROOKS	DENNIS	26	.00	Lewiston	ME
857	BROOKS	ELI	19	15.00	Carolina Landing	MS
928	BROOKS	JOHN	27	15.00	Carolina Landing	MS
281	BROOKS	MARY	21	6.00	Millersville	MD
282	BROOKS	NANCY	4	.00	Millersville	MD
748	BROOKS	WILLIAM L.	18	12.00	Helena	AR
316	BROWN	ALBERT	8	.00	Millersville	MD
326	BROWN	BENJAMIN	22	8.33	Millersville	MD
553	BROWN	BOB	20	8.00	Canton	MS
1139	BROWN	DAVID	28	.00	Philadelphia	PA
701	BROWN	DICK	21	12.00	Helena	AR
473	BROWN	HENRY	29	12.00	Vicksburgh	MS
1043	BROWN	HENRY	25	15.00	Lake Providence	LA
1108	BROWN	HENRY	19	.00	Baltimore	MD
1136	BROWN	HENRY	34	.00	Philadelphia	PA
141	BROWN	ISAAC	35	8.00	Millersville	MD

314	BROWN	LUCIUS	25	8.33	Millersville	MD
766	BROWN	MRS. WILLIAM	24	9.00	Carolina Landing	MS
871	BROWN	NANCY	28	9.00	Carolina Landing	MS
290	BROWN	NED	10	.00	Port Tobacco	MD
261	BROWN	ROBERT	24	12.00	Relay House	MD
623	BROWN	ROBERT	27	8.00	Crownsville	MD
869	BROWN	S.	32	15.00	Carolina Landing	MS
315	BROWN	SARAH	20	5.00	Millersville	MD
54	BROWN	SOL	19	.00	Hoods Mill	MD
719	BROWN	THOMAS	21	12.00	Helena	AR
283	BROWN	WILLIAM	14	2.50	Dunkirk	MD
765	BROWN	WILLIAM	28	15.00	Carolina Landing	MS
1110	BROWN	WILLIAM	31	.00	Baltimore	MD
1135	BROWN	WILLIAM	26	.00	Philadelphia	PA
234	BRYANT	CLARA	21	.00	Piscataway	MD
233	BRYANT	THOMAS	29	9.17	Piscataway	MD
590	BULLARD	AARON	28	10.00	Canton	MS
761	BULLARD	JOHN	21	15.00	Carolina Landing	MS
1111	BUMFRY*	WALTER	33	.00	Baltimore	MD
922	BURK	LASCON*	24	15.00	Carolina Landing	MS
13	BURLEY	GEORGE	26	10.00	Olney	MD
1098	BURLEY	WILLIAM	25	.00	Baltimore	MD
935	BURRIS	THOMAS	24	15.00	Carolina Landing	MS
690	BURTON	RICHARD	24	10.00	Bladensburg	MD
876	BUSH	EPHRAIM	36	15.00	Carolina Landing	MS
1072	BUSH	HENRY	32	15.00	Lake Providence	LA
1010	BUSH	WILLIAM	30	15.00	Lake Providence	LA
813	BUTLER	BENJAMIN	28	15.00	Carolina Landing	MS
477	BUTLER	BENJAMIN F.	21	12.00	Vicksburgh	MS
969	BUTLER	CLARA	29	9.00	Carolina Landing	MS
289	BUTLER	JOHN	19	8.00	Port Tobacco	MD
617	BUTLER	WILLIAM	12	1.00	Rutland	MD
949	BUTLER	WILLIAM	17	10.00	Carolina Landing	MS
559	BUTTON	WILLIAM	36	10.00	Canton	MS
346	CAMBRIDGE	ELIZABETH	20	5.00	Millersville	MD
345	CAMBRIDGE	JOHN	30	9.00	Millersville	MD
181	CAMPBELL	JOHN	30	.00	Upper Marlboro	MD
1090	CAPMAN	MARY	18	.00	Philadelphia	PA
140	CAREY	JAMES	25	8.33	Anne Arundel Co.	MD
782	CARNETT	ANNA	32	9.00	Carolina Landing	MS
784	CARNETT	JAMES	10	.00	Carolina Landing	MS
786	CARNETT	JAMES	36	15.00	Carolina Landing	MS
783	CARNETT	JOHN	12	.00	Carolina Landing	MS
785	CARNETT	NANCY	8	.00	Carolina Landing	MS
404	CARR	JAMES	26	10.00	Upper Marlboro	MD
1024	CARROLE	EDWARD	26	15.00	Lake Providence	LA
461	CARROLL	CHAVIS	21	12.00	Vicksburgh	MS
498	CARTER	ALLEN	24	8.00	Port Tobacco	MD
582	CARTER	CAROLINE	18	6.00	Canton	MS
499	CARTER	ELLEN	19	3.50	Port Tobacco	MD
901	CARTER	GEORGE	28	15.00	Carolina Landing	MS
882	CARTER	HARRIS	32	15.00	Carolina Landing	MS
884	CARTER	JAMES	19	15.00	Carolina Landing	MS
1140	CARTER	JAMES H.	19	.00	Philadelphia	PA
1086	CARTER	LEWIS	24	.00	Philadelphia	PA
505	CARTER	RICHARD	18	5.00	Port Tobacco	MD
236	CARTER	ROSANNA	28	6.00	Annapolis	MD

595	CARTER	WILLIAM	28	10.00	Canton	MS
77	CARTER	WILSON	25	.00	Hoods Mill	MD
751	CATTON	CHARLES	28	12.00	Helena	AR
734	CAWKINS	ALICK	14	5.00	Helena	AR
1145	CHAMBERLIN	JULIUS	21	.00	Philadelphia	PA
311	CHAPMAN	ANNA	20	.00	Warrenton	VA
309	CHAPMAN	HENRY	25	10.00	Warrenton	VA
737	CHAPMAN	JOHN	31	12.00	Helena	AR
106	CHECKS	BRISTOE	58	5.83	Carroll Co.	MD
109	CHECKS	CATHERINE	8	.00	Carroll Co.	MD
110	CHECKS	MIDA	4	.00	Carroll Co.	MD
107	CHECKS	SOPHY	45	4.16	Carroll Co.	MD
108	CHECKS*	AMELIA	14	3.50	Carroll Co.	MD
603	CHEESEMAN	HENRY	28	8.00	Millersville	MD
397	CHILTON	JACOB	15	5.00	Allens Fresh	MD
47	CHRISTEN	KATE	28	.00	Poplar Springs	MD
48	CHRISTEN	SUSAN	9	.00	Poplar Springs	MD
46	CHRISTEN	WILLIAM	35	10.00	Poplar Springs	MD
49	CHRISTEN	WILLIAM B.	1	.00	Poplar Springs	MD
573	CLARK	BENJAMIN	25	10.00	Canton	MS
1121	CLARK	HENRY	30	.00	Baltimore	MD
40	CLARK	JOSEPH	22	10.00	Matthews Store	MD
453	CLARK	SUSANNAH	20	6.00	Princeton	NJ
756	CLARK	WILLIAM	26	15.00	Carolina Landing	MS
1091	CLARK	WILLIAM	24	.00	Philadelphia	PA
52	CLAYBORNE	ANDERSON	21	.00	Hoods Mill	MD
679	CLAYBORNE	PEGGY	30	6.00	Bladensburg	MD
515	CLOUD	ALMA	30	.00	Clarksville	MD
516	CLOUD	JENNIE	6	.00	Clarksville	MD
517	CLOUD	JOHN	4	.00	Clarksville	MD
514	CLOUD	THOMAS	42	10.00	Clarksville	MD
390	CMITH	CHARLES	28	9.00	Allens Fresh	MD
793	COATS	JOHN	24	15.00	Carolina Landing	MS
633	COFFEE	ALEXANDER	19	7.00	Allens Fresh	MD
232	COLEMAN	HANNAH	21	7.00	Simpsonville	MD
500	COLEMAN	JERRY	44	10.00	Upper Marlboro	MD
503	COLEMAN	LAWSON	16	3.33	Upper Marlboro	MD
501	COLEMAN	NELLIE	36	.00	Upper Marlboro	MD
504	COLEMAN	SAMUEL W.	15	3.33	Upper Marlboro	MD
231	COLEMAN	WILLIAM	26	10.00	Simpsonville	MD
830	COLEMAN	WILLIAM	38	15.00	Carolina Landing	MS
502	COLEMAN	ZACK	17	3.33	Upper Marlboro	MD
619	COLES	BAKER	21	10.00	Hillsboro	VA
977	COLES	JOHN	8	.00	Carolina Landing	MS
976	COLES	MANUEL	26	15.00	Carolina Landing	MS
796	COLLIER	JOHN	30	15.00	Carolina Landing	MS
903	COLLINS	WILLIAM	40	15.00	Carolina Landing	MS
566	COLSON	JAMES	31	10.00	Canton	MS
63	CONWAY	EUSTED	20	10.00	Trenton	NJ
657	CONWAY	JOHN	30	10.00	Bladensburg	MD
351	COOK	MAT	48	8.33	Millersville	MD
695	COOPER	MATTHEW	24	12.00	Saint Denis	MD
1013	COORS	JAMES	22	15.00	Lake Providence	LA
319	CORBIN	MASON	12	5.00	Millersville	MD
1103	CORRALL*	WILLIAM	21	.00	Baltimore	MD
579	COTTON	FLEMING	31	12.00	Canton	MS
625	COTTON	HENRY	19	8.33	Millersville	MD

324	COURTENY	WILLIAM	24	8.00	Millersville	MD
166	COVINGTON	BEDFORD	19	10.00	King George	VA
534	COVINGTON	GERARDSON	46	10.00	Canton	MS
531	COVINGTON	GRANDISON	20	8.00	Friendship	MD
535	COVINGTON	HARRIETTE	40	8.00	Canton	MS
538	COVINGTON	JOHN H.	16	6.00	Canton	MS
405	COVINGTON	PHILIP	28	8.00	West River	MD
536	COVINGTON	ROSE	18	4.00	Canton	MS
537	COVINGTON*	LAUREN	14	2.00	Canton	MS
1012	COWAN	WILLIAM	19	15.00	Lake Providence	LA
244	CRAIG	JANE	29	7.00	Warren Co.	PA
950	CRAMP	AUSTIN	27	15.00	Carolina Landing	MS
103	CRAWFORD	MINOR	13	7.00	Middlesex	NJ
1134	CRAWLEY	WILLIAM C.	21	.00	Philadelphia	PA
746	CROSS	CRUTCHWELL	21	12.00	Helena	AR
652	CROSS	JAMES	14	4.00	Collington	MD
1128	CROSS	ROBERT	24	.00	Lewiston	ME
45	CRUTCHFIELD	ASHBY	20	10.00	Poplar Springs	MD
162	CURTIS	OVERTON	25	20.00	Waterford	PA
235	CURTIS	RICHARD	38	10.00	Annapolis	MD
240	CUSTIS	HENRY	26	10.00	Allens Fresh	MD
241	CUSTIS	MARTHA	24	.00	Allens Fresh	MD
554	DAGGS	WILLIAM	16	6.00	Canton	MS
555	DAGGS	WILLIAM N.	14	4.00	Canton	MS
1115	DAHL	SAMUEL	22	.00	Baltimore	MD
100	DANIELS	ELLIS	25	10.00	Middlesex	NJ
1112	DANIELS	EPHRAIM	27	.00	Baltimore	MD
94	DANIELS	WILLIAM	24	25.00	Acquia Creek Land.	MD
920	DAVIS	ALVIN	26	15.00	Carolina Landing	MS
1125	DAVIS	ANDREW	31	.00	Lewiston	ME
656	DAVIS	ANNA	20	4.00	Dyers Mills	VA
173	DAVIS	HENRY	20	7.00	Howard Co.	MD
655	DAVIS	HENRY	26	8.00	Dyers Mills	VA
910	DAVIS	ORAN	27	15.00	Carolina Landing	MS
620	DAVIS	SAMUEL	28	10.00	Hillsboro	VA
21	DAVIS	THOMAS	21	10.00	Hoods Mill	MD
356	DAVIS	WILLIAM	19	6.75	Bryantown	MD
1126	DAVIS	WILLIAM	33	.00	Lewiston	ME
720	DAVIS	WILLIAM H.	19	12.00	Helena	AR
57	DAY	JUNIUS	29	.00	Hoods Mill	MD
99	DEAN	HENRY	42	12.00	Middlesex	NJ
981	DEAN	WILLIAM H.	21	8.00	Woodstock	MD
361	DELANCY	MARY	19	8.00	Warrenton	VA
67	DEMING	JOHN	29	10.00	Davidsonville	MD
52	DENNIS	ISAIAH	26	.00	Hoods Mill	MD
434	DENNISON	JAMES	34	.00	Edgehill	VA
921	DERENDOFF	JOHN	27	15.00	Carolina Landing	MS
1032	DEVILLY	JOHN	20	15.00	Lake Providence	LA
985	DICKS	HENRY	12	2.00	Silver Hill	MD
681	DICKSON	ANDREW	19	10.00	Crownsville	MD
636	DIGGS	JAMES	24	9.00	Prince Frederick	MD
927	DIGGS	JOHN	28	15.00	Carolina Landing	MS
342	DILLIVER	DAVID	24	8.33	Baltimore	MD
343	DILLIVER	MELVINA	18	6.00	Baltimore	MD
997	DIXON	GEORGE	24	15.00	Lake Providence	LA
527	DODSON	WATT	21	6.25	Bryantown	MD
213	DORE	WOODWARD	41	10.00	Brooks Station	MD

942	DORSEY	ED	21	15.00	Carolina Landing	MS
646	DORSEY	RICHARD	25	8.00	Newburg	MD
669	DORSEY	RICHARD	24	9.00	Port Tobacco	MD
647	DORSEY	SAMUEL	26	8.00	Newburg	MD
631	DOUGAL	FRANK	26	6.67	Bryantown	MD
398	DOUGLAS	CAROLINE	22	8.00	Ardwick	MD
35	DOUGLAS	FRED	19	5.00	Freedom	MD
429	DOUGLAS	WILLIAM	24	10.00	Crownsville	MD
893	DOUGLAS	WILLIAM	28	15.00	Carolina Landing	MS
171	DOW	JAMES	26	12.00	Baltimore	MD
224	DREWITE*	HUMPHREY	26	10.00	Johnsons Store	MD
1016	DREWRY	HUMPHREY	24	15.00	Lake Providence	LA
313	DRIVER	SAMUEL	28	10.00	Annapolis	MD
1117	DUVALL	SAMUEL	18	.00	Baltimore	MD
630	EATON	JOHN	25	5.00	Allens Fresh	MD
381	ECKLY	JOHN	20	8.33	Aquasco	MD
874	EDMONDSON	JOHN	28	15.00	Carolina Landing	MS
193	EDWARD	JAMES	24	9.17	Aquasco	MD
965	EDWARDS	EDWARD	30	15.00	Carolina Landing	MS
280	ELDRIDGE	GEORGE	30	10.00	Millersville	MD
457	ELLINGTON	ROBERT	15	.00	Jefferson Co.	IL
372	ELLIS	JAKE	24	9.17	Aquasco	MD
81	ELLIS	JOHN	49	8.00	Marriottsville	MD
520	ELLIS	JOHN	10	.00	Port Tobacco	MD
91	EPPS	PETER	18	25.00	Acquia Creek Land.	MD
387	EVANS	DAVID	13	.00	Millersville	MD
971	EVANS	HENRY	14	8.00	Carolina Landing	MS
375	EVANS	JAMES	24	9.17	Aquasco	MD
27	FARROW	GEORGE	20	10.00	Hoods Mill	MD
762	FAY	GEORGE	21	15.00	Carolina Landing	MS
919	FELTON	HENRY	24	15.00	Carolina Landing	MS
686	FIELD	ANDREW	30	8.00	Prince Frederick	MD
924	FIELDHAM	SAMUEL	16	9.00	Carolina Landing	MS
89	FINDLEY	WILLIAM	30	25.00	Acquia Creek Land.	MD
583	FITZHUGH	AGNES	27	6.00	Canton	MS
584	FITZHUGH	MARY	2	.00	Canton	MS
1088	FLANAGAN	ANN	20	.00	Philadelphia	PA
1044	FLECK	EDWARD	30	15.00	Lake Providence	LA
661	FLETCHER	GOVENOR	13	.00	St. Johnsville	NY
564	FLETCHER	ROBERT	26	10.00	Canton	MS
991	FORBES	THOMAS	26	10.00	Egg Harbor	NJ
581	FORD	CHARLES	20	8.00	Canton	MS
528	FORD	JAMES	12	3.75	Bryantown	MD
973	FORD	SYLVESTER	29	15.00	Carolina Landing	MS
558	FORD	WILLIAM	21	8.00	Canton	MS
439	FOWLES*	JOHN	22	.00	Edgehill	VA
161	FRANCIS	JOHN	30	20.00	Waterford	PA
4	FRANKLIN	BENJAMIN	28	10.00	Montgomery Co.	MD
742	FRANKLIN	BENJAMIN	26	12.00	Helena	AR
799	FRANKLIN	ISAAC	16	11.00	Carolina Landing	MS
478	FRANKLIN	ROBERT	18	12.00	Vicksburgh	MS
731	FRANKLIN	ROBERT	24	12.00	Helena	AR
809	FRANKLIN	ROBERT	30	15.00	Carolina Landing	MS
188	FRANKLIN	THOMAS	37	9.17	Anne Arundel Co.	MD
79	FRANKLIN	WILLIAM	16	5.00	Collington	MD
529	FREEMAN	FRANK	24	8.00	Friendship	MD
2	FREEMAN	MATT	24	10.00	Montgomery Co.	MD

113	FULTON	EDWARD	21	10.00	Prince Georges Co.	MD
304	GADLEY	EDMUND	24	10.00	Bealton	MD
787	GAINES	PETER	21	15.00	Carolina Landing	MS
125	GAINES	THORNTON	45	10.00	Millersville	MD
845	GAMBOL	R. H.	18	15.00	Carolina Landing	MS
877	GAMBROLE	FANNIE	24	9.00	Carolina Landing	MS
688	GANS	NELSON	24	12.00	Cleveland	OH
182	GANTRY*	PETER	40	.00	Upper Marlboro	MD
894	GARDEN	WALTER	30	15.00	Carolina Landing	MS
325	GARDNER	ADAM	26	8.33	Millersville	MD
867	GARDNER	JANE	21	9.00	Carolina Landing	MS
629	GARY*	JAMES	26	4.17	Bryantown	MD
418	GATEFOOD	JARED	29	8.33	Pamunkey	MD
892	GATEWOOD	JACOB	36	15.00	Carolina Landing	MS
115	GATEWOOD	JANE	15	6.00	Howard Co.	MD
479	GATEWOOD	JARED	40	12.00	Vicksburgh	MS
512	GAY	HENRY	29	8.33	Occoquan	VA
1077	GEORGE	CHURCHILL	24	.00	Philadelphia	PA
312	GHAPMAN	JENNIE	4	.00	Warrenton	VA
987	GIBBONS	WILLIAM H.	13	1.00	Allentown	PA
179	GIBBS	JAMES	21	.00	Upper Marlboro	MD
906	GIBSON	HENRY	19	15.00	Carolina Landing	MS
101	GIBSON	ISAAC	25	12.00	Middlesex	NJ
1027	GIBSON	JOHN	19	15.00	Lake Providence	LA
1107	GIBSON	SAMUEL	18	.00	Baltimore	MD
456	GIFTS	JAMES	25	12.00	Princeton	NJ
446	GILBERT	HARRISON	13	6.00	Rockspring	PA
330	GILMAN	ISAAC	16	7.00	Millersville	MD
1052	GOODING	HENRY	34	15.00	Lake Providence	LA
61	GORDON	ALFRED	31	.00	Hoods Mill	MD
667	GORDON	ELIJAH	24	10.00	Beltsville	MD
855	GORDON	THORNTON	28	15.00	Carolina Landing	MS
447	GORDON	W.	30	10.00	Bradensburg	MD
930	GRADING*	ROBERT	14	6.00	Carolina Landing	MS
423	GRADY	JACOB	26	10.00	Shepardstown	MD
578	GRANDY	WILLIS	28	10.00	Canton	MS
206	GRANT	HENRY	29	9.17	Aquasco	MD
215	GRANT	HENRY	36	8.33	Prince Georges Co.	MD
279	GRANT	HENRY	28	8.00	Rockville	MD
307	GRANT	HENRY	24	8.00	West River	MD
237	GRAY	ISAIAH	36	10.00	Orangeville	MD
1067	GRAY	JAMES	30	15.00	Lake Providence	LA
689	GRAY	JOHN	28	12.00	Cleveland	OH
895	GRAY	NICHOLAS	20	15.00	Carolina Landing	MS
238	GRAY	REBECCA	23	6.00	Orangeville	MD
440	GRAYSON	DANIEL	26	15.00	Edgehill	VA
863	GREEN	ALMSTED	24	15.00	Carolina Landing	MS
827	GREEN	DANUEL	19	15.00	Carolina Landing	MS
805	GREEN	FRANCIS	19	9.00	Carolina Landing	MS
702	GREEN	GEORGE	19	12.00	Helena	AR
1065	GREEN	MARCELLUS	19	15.00	Lake Providence	LA
846	GREEN	MARILLUS	21	115.0	Carolina Landing	MS
111	GREEN	SAMUEL	25	10.00	Marriottsville	MD
841	GREEN	SAMUEL	19	15.00	Carolina Landing	MS
1057	GREEN	SAMUEL	26	15.00	Lake Providence	LA
133	GRICE	PHOEBE	70	.00	Bladensburg	MD
112	GRIFFIN	GEORGE	25	10.00	Marriottsville	MD

1015	GRIFFIN	JAMES	30	15.00	Lake Providence	LA
145	GROSIER	JAMES	19	8.00	Crownsville	MD
144	GROSIER	MOSES	49	8.00	Crownsville	MD
142	GROSIER	WASHINGTON	57	8.00	Millersville	MD
288	GUENTHER	HARRY	29	8.00	Port Tobacco	MD
32	GUSTUS	HENRY	23	10.00	Hoods Mill	MD
1095	HALE	ELSON	27	.00	Philadelphia	PA
1084	HALE	JOSHUA	32	.00	Philadelphia	PA
464	HALLIDAY	FRANK	26	12.00	Vicksburgh	MS
424	HALLUM	NAT	30	10.00	Shepardstown	MD
71	HAMBLIN	DAVID	19	.00	Hoods Mill	MD
911	HAMILTON	THOMAS	24	15.00	Carolina Landing	MS
465	HAMPTON	WADE	21	12.00	Vicksburgh	MS
645	HAMPTON	WADE	24	9.00	Newburg	MD
1000	HANCOCK	JAMES	13	7.00	Lake Providence	LA
576	HANES*	ROBERT	17	6.00	Canton	MS
714	HANNETT	ROBERT	24	12.00	Helena	AR
399	HANSON	JOHN H.	21	8.33	Bryantown	MD
160	HARNES	ANTHONY	27	30.00	Waterford	PA
211	HARRIS	BEVERLY	28	10.00	Montgomery Co.	MD
519	HARRIS	GEORGE	9	.00	Port Tobacco	MD
898	HARRIS	JACOB	16	8.00	Carolina Landing	MS
58	HARRIS	JESSIE	31	.00	Hoods Mill	MD
302	HARRIS	JOHN	24	9.17	Aquasco	MD
481	HARRIS	JOSEPH	24	12.00	Vicksburgh	MS
627	HARRIS	SOPHY	19	5.00	Indiana Co.	PA
196	HARRISON	ANNA	39	4.00	Ellicott Mills	MD
197	HARRISON	JENNIE	12	.00	Ellicott Mills	MD
195	HARRISON	THOMAS	46	8.00	Ellicott Mills	MD
626	HARRISON	THOMAS	21	13.00	Indiana Co.	PA
198	HARRISON	TOM	4	.00	Ellicott Mills	MD
727	HARRISON	WILLIAM	28	12.00	Helena	AR
993	HARVEY	WILLIAM	37	10.00	Little Gunpowder	MD
225	HAULSTON	HENRY	13	.00	Rahway	NJ
995	HAWKINS	FANNY	24	5.00	Satansville	MD
996	HAWKINS	JOHN	6	.00	Satansville	MD
844	HAWKINS	JOHN H.	20	15.00	Carolina Landing	MS
248	HAWKINS	NICHOLAS	28	8.00	Hoopersville	MD
994	HAWKINS	WILLIAM	30	10.00	Satansville	MD
31	HAWLEY	ANTHONY	19	10.00	Hoods Mill	MD
752	HAWLEY	MARTIN	27	12.00	Helena	AR
1058	HAWLEY	TOBIAS	20	15.00	Lake Providence	LA
726	HEDGES	WILLIAM	24	12.00	Helena	AR
571	HENDERSON	HENRY C.	38	10.00	Canton	MS
1022	HENRY	JOHN	23	15.00	Lake Providence	LA
1095	HENRY	JOHN	22	.00	Baltimore	MD
941	HENRY	JOHN W.	34	15.00	Carolina Landing	MS
908	HENRY	MARTIN	20	15.00	Carolina Landing	MS
1003	HENRY	MARTIN	26	15.00	Lake Providence	LA
750	HENRY	PHILIP	31	12.00	Helena	AR
946	HENRY	SAMUEL	27	15.00	Carolina Landing	MS
1059	HENRY	SAMUEL	27	15.00	Lake Providence	LA
1132	HENRY	SAMUEL	21	.00	Philadelphia	PA
451	HENRY	WILLIAM	28	12.00	Cleveland	OH
545	HENRY	WILLIAM	30	10.00	Canton	MS
703	HENSON*	SAMUEL	26	12.00	Helena	AR
349	HERBERT	ARCHY	28	8.33	Mt. Gillman	VA

350	HERBERT	HARRIETTE	20	1.25	Mt. Gillman	VA
116	HEROD	AMEL	30	12.00	Prince Georges Co.	MD
117	HEROD	CLARISSA	30	7.00	Prince Georges Co.	MD
371	HEROD	WILLIAM	22	7.50	Allens Fresh	MD
615	HEROD	WILLIAM	24	10.00	Annapolis	MD
12	HEROLD	JOHN	29	10.00	Hoods Mill	MD
684	HICKMAN	LEWIS	25	10.00	Hillsboro	VA
936	HICKS	CHARLES W.	22	15.00	Carolina Landing	MS
859	HIGGINS	WILLIAM	22	15.00	Carolina Landing	MS
64	HILE	HENRY	23	10.00	Trenton	NJ
574	HILL	BENJAMIN	26	10.00	Canton	MS
357	HILL	GEORGE	26	8.33	Allens Fresh	MD
368	HILL	GEORGE	32	9.33	Davidsonville	MD
358	HILL	HARRIETTE	22	3.33	Allens Fresh	MD
369	HILL	HARRIETTE	22	5.00	Davidsonville	MD
541	HILL	HENRY	20	8.00	Canton	MS
909	HILL	HENRY	30	15.00	Carolina Landing	MS
359	HILL	JANNIE	10	.00	Allens Fresh	MD
493	HILL	NANCY	4	12.00	Vicksburgh	MS
44	HILL	NAT	16	1.50	Millersville	MD
492	HILL	RACHAEL	24	8.00	Vicksburgh	MS
801	HOBSON	SAMUEL	24	15.00	Carolina Landing	MS
170	HOGANS	NISLY	19	12.00	Baltimore	MD
17	HOLMES	JAMES	31	10.00	Hoods Mill	MD
320	HOLMES	JULIA	18	2.25	Millersville	MD
980	HOLMES	MAJOR	22	12.00	Westmoreland Co.	VA
759	HOPKINS	ELVIRA	19	9.00	Carolina Landing	MS
749	HOPKINS	ROBERT	19	12.00	Helena	AR
814	HOUSE	CHARLES	20	15.00	Carolina Landing	MS
580	HOWARD	EDWARD	29	10.00	Canton	MS
242	HOWARD	JAMES	23	9.00	Allens Fresh	MD
1036	HOWDON*	SAMUEL	26	15.00	Lake Providence	LA
153	HUGHES	WILLIAM	29	12.00	Somersett	MD
183	HUNTER	ROBERT	28	.00	Upper Marlboro	MD
642	HURLEY	WILLIAM	20	8.00	Huntingtown	MD
226	INGRAHAM	JOHN	26	8.00	Montgomery Co.	MD
33	IRVIN	JAMES	19	10.00	Hoods Mill	MD
1020	JACKSON	ALFRED	16	10.00	Lake Providence	LA
710	JACKSON	ANDREW	24	12.00	Helena	AR
744	JACKSON	ANDREW	21	12.00	Helena	AR
738	JACKSON	BENJAMIN	24	12.00	Helena	AR
700	JACKSON	BEVERLY	30	12.00	Helena	AR
42	JACKSON	DENNIS	17	7.00	Millersville	MD
543	JACKSON	DENNIS	14	6.00	Canton	MS
382	JACKSON	EDWARD	26	9.17	Aquasco	MD
599	JACKSON	GEORGE	30	10.00	Millersville	MD
732	JACKSON	HERBERT	26	12.00	Helena	AR
176	JACKSON	JAMES	26	.00	Upper Marlboro	MD
670	JACKSON	JAMES	30	9.00	Port Tobacco	MD
869	JACKSON	JAMES	19	15.00	Carolina Landing	MS
896	JACKSON	JAMES	32	15.00	Carolina Landing	MS
1019	JACKSON	JAMES R.	28	15.00	Lake Providence	LA
1073	JACKSON	LANDON	21	15.00	Lake Providence	LA
1055	JACKSON	LEWIS	19	15.00	Lake Providence	LA
177	JACKSON	MADISON	20	.00	Upper Marlboro	MD
452	JACKSON	MADISON	28	12.00	Princeton	NJ
62	JACKSON	PETER	30	10.00	Trenton	NJ

547	JACKSON	PETER	24	10.00	Canton	MS
472	JACKSON	SAMUEL	19	12.00	Vicksburgh	MS
1017	JACKSON	SAMUEL	22	15.00	Lake Providence	LA
1034	JACKSON	SARAH	16	10.00	Lake Providence	LA
104	JACKSON	THORNTON	26	9.00	Howard Co.	MD
216	JACKSON	WARNER	29	10.00	Baltimore	MD
263	JACKSON	WILLIAM	16	6.00	Relay House	MD
256	JAMES	AGNES	24	6.00	Marriottsville	MD
90	JAMES	ANDREW	24	25.00	Acquia Creek Land.	MD
792	JAMES	JOHN	26	15.00	Carolina Landing	MS
257	JAMES	SARAH	16	2.00	Marriottsville	MD
256	JAMES	SIMON	36	12.00	Marriottsville	MD
715	JAMES	WILLIAM	21	12.00	Helena	AR
865	JAMES	WILLIAM	26	15.00	Carolina Landing	MS
114	JAMES	WORTHAL	17	8.00	Howard Co.	MD
542	JASPER	WILLIAM	26	10.00	Canton	MS
687	JAVIX*	CLARA	18	6.00	Uniontown	PA
1053	JEFFERSON	THOMAS	24	15.00	Lake Providence	LA
934	JEFFIRES	PINKLEY	19	15.00	Carolina Landing	MS
13	JENKING	HENRY	20	10.00	Hoods Mill	MD
718	JENKINS	ROBERT	30	12.00	Helena	AR
362	JENNIFER	WARREN	10	.00	Warrenton	VA
692	JOHNSON	ABRAM	26	10.00	South River	MD
982	JOHNSON	ALBERT	20	10.00	Allentown	PA
758	JOHNSON	ALFRED	21	15.00	Carolina Landing	MS
904	JOHNSON	ARCHY	28	15.00	Carolina Landing	MS
810	JOHNSON	ARTHUR	21	15.00	Carolina Landing	MS
862	JOHNSON	ASHBY	26	15.00	Carolina Landing	MS
546	JOHNSON	BUCK	28	10.00	Canton	MS
412	JOHNSON	CHARLES	36	10.00	Millersville	MD
851	JOHNSON	CHARLES	25	15.00	Carolina Landing	MS
69	JOHNSON	DANIEL	30	.00	Hoods Mill	MD
60	JOHNSON	GEORGE	29	.00	Hoods Mill	MD
327	JOHNSON	GEORGINA	18	4.00	Millersville	MD
132	JOHNSON	GRACE	6	.00	Bladensburg	MD
260	JOHNSON	GUY	36	12.00	Relay House	MD
129	JOHNSON	HANNAH	41	8.00	Bladensburg	MD
854	JOHNSON	HENRY	24	15.00	Carolina Landing	MS
728	JOHNSON	HENRY J.	31	12.00	Helena	AR
883	JOHNSON	ISAAC	26	15.00	Carolina Landing	MS
131	JOHNSON	JACOB	8	.00	Bladensburg	MD
414	JOHNSON	JEANIE	8	.00	Millersville	MD
1120	JOHNSON	JESSE	19	.00	Baltimore	MD
102	JOHNSON	JOHN	22	10.00	Middlesex	NJ
480	JOHNSON	JOHN	32	12.00	Vicksburgh	MS
712	JOHNSON	JOHN	25	12.00	Helena	AR
806	JOHNSON	JOHN	23	15.00	Carolina Landing	MS
1082	JOHNSON	JOHN	22	.00	Philadelphia	PA
380	JOHNSON	JOHN H.	25	9.17	Aquasco	MD
922	JOHNSON	JOSEPH	27	15.00	Carolina Landing	MS
259	JOHNSON	JOSH	14	5.00	Allens Fresh	MD
231	JOHNSON	JULIA	21	5.00	Freetown	MD
413	JOHNSON	LUCY	26	5.00	Millersville	MD
824	JOHNSON	PETER	22	15.00	Carolina Landing	MS
130	JOHNSON	PHOEBE	15	6.00	Bladensburg	MD
318	JOHNSON	REUBEN	28	8.33	Millersville	MD
1081	JOHNSON	RICHARD	19	.00	Philadelphia	PA

202	JOHNSON	ROBERT	19	9.17	Aquasco	MD
518	JOHNSON	ROBERT	36	8.00	Port Tobacco	MD
551	JOHNSON	ROBERT	18	8.00	Canton	MS
662	JOHNSON	ROBERT	24	6.00	Newburg	MD
775	JOHNSON	ROBERT	40	15.00	Carolina Landing	MS
899	JOHNSON	ROBERT	27	15.00	Carolina Landing	MS
223	JOHNSON	SAMUEL	26	10.00	Queenstown	MD
706	JOHNSON	SAMUEL	28	12.00	Helena	AR
939	JOHNSON	THAD	29	15.00	Carolina Landing	MS
525	JOHNSON	THOMAS	8	.00	Rutland	MD
848	JOHNSON	THOMAS	27	15.00	Carolina Landing	MS
624	JOHNSON	TOBY	14	.00	Millersville	MD
880	JOHNSON	WALTER	31	15.00	Carolina Landing	MS
526	JOHNSON	WILLIAM	19	5.00	Bryantown	MD
839	JOHNSON	WILLIAM	20	15.00	Carolina Landing	MS
858	JOHNSON	WILLIAM	30	15.00	Carolina Landing	MS
1106	JOHNSON	WILLIAM	20	.00	Baltimore	MD
693	JOHNSON	WILLIAM W.	24	10.00	South River	MD
415	JOHNSON	WILLIE	4	.00	Millersville	MD
897	JOHNSON	WILLIS	34	15.00	Carolina Landing	MS
443	JONES	ADAM	30	12.00	Lehigh	PA
788	JONES	ALEX	26	15.00	Carolina Landing	MS
168	JONES	ANN	24	5.00	King George	VA
41	JONES	CARTER	19	8.00	Millersville	MD
1083	JONES	CHARLES	30	.00	Philadelphis	PA
933	JONES	HAMILTON	42	15.00	Carolina Landing	MS
66	JONES	ISAAC	23	10.00	Davidsonville	MD
958	JONES	LEWIS	15	8.00	Carolina Landing	MS
365	JONES	MARIA	22	5.00	Savage	MD
957	JONES	MARIE	26	9.00	Carolina Landing	MS
607	JONES	MILTON	10	.00	Allens Fresh	MD
1026	JONES	WILLIAM	19	15.00	Lake Providence	LA
713	JONES	WILLIAM H.	23	12.00	Helena	AR
460	JORDAN	PETER	22	12.00	Vicksburgh	MS
779	JOYCE	ALLEN	8	.00	Carolina Landing	MS
777	JOYCE	FRANCIS	30	9.00	Carolina Landing	MS
866	JOYCE	JAMES	28	15.00	Carolina Landing	MS
778	JOYCE	NANCY	10	.00	Carolina Landing	MS
780	JOYCE	PETER	6	.00	Carolina Landing	MS
812	JUST	WILLIAM	26	15.00	Carolina Landing	MS
1144	KANE	SOPHIA	22	.00	Philadelphia	PA
55	KELLER	RAYMOND	21	.00	Hoods Mill	MD
565	KENNEY	JAMES	28	12.00	Canton	MS
360	KENNY	HANNAH E.	16	2.50	Baltimore	MD
147	KENT	ABRAM	22	12.00	Havre De Grace	MD
148	KENT	RACHEL	26	6.00	Havre De Grace	MD
827	KERR	ALBERT	10	.00	Carolina Landing	MS
828	KERR	JAMES	8	.00	Carolina Landing	MS
829	KERR	MARY	4	.00	Carolina Landing	MS
826	KERR	SUSANNAH	26	9.00	Carolina Landing	MS
831	KERR	WILSON	29	15.00	Carolina Landing	MS
637	KEY	CALVIN	24	9.00	Huntingtown	MD
136	KEY	SOL	23	15.00	Anne Arundel Co.	MD
951	KING	GEORGE E.	29	15.00	Carolina Landing	MS
1078	KING	HENRY	26	.00	Philadelphia	PA
676	KING	JOHN	24	10.00	Arnolds Store	MD
959	KING	JOSEPH	36	15.00	Carolina Landing	MS

1138	KING	SAMUEL	31	.00	Philadelphia	PA
721	KINSDALE	JOHN	24	12.00	Helena	AR
354	LABOR*	THOMAS	16	5.00	Charlotte Hall	MD
243	LANCASTER	JOHN	50	10.00	Allens Fresh	MD
605	LANCASTER	JOHN	54	10.00	Millersville	MD
606	LANCASTER,JR	JOHN	14	5.00	Millersville	MD
420	LANDEN	TRAVERSE	24	7.00	Little Gunpowder	MD
539	LAWSON	TRAVERSE	29	12.00	Canton	MS
87	LEE	EDWARD	26	10.00	Hoods Mill	MD
945	LEE	HENRY	19	15.00	Carolina Landing	MS
1030	LEE	JAMES	36	15.00	Lake Providence	LA
1113	LEMON*	JOHN	24	.00	Baltimore	MD
274	LEWIS	ALEXANDER	46	10.00	Fauquier Co.	VA
333	LEWIS	ANNA	20	.00	Bladensburg	MD
51	LEWIS	BENJAMIN	24	.00	Hoods Mill	MD
445	LEWIS	ELIJAH	19	10.00	Lehigh	PA
675	LEWIS	HENRY	21	10.00	Huntingtown	MD
685	LEWIS	HENRY	26	8.00	Prince Frederick	MD
840	LEWIS	HENRY	26	15.00	Carolina Landing	MS
407	LEWIS	ISAAC	26	8.33	Ellicott Mills	MD
411	LEWIS	JAMES	16	6.25	Bristol	MD
593	LEWIS	JAMES	29	10.00	Canton	MS
336	LEWIS	JENNIE	3	.00	Bladensburg	MD
335	LEWIS	JOHN	4	.00	Bladensburg	MD
937	LEWIS	JOHN	40	15.00	Carolina Landing	MS
334	LEWIS	PETER	6	.00	Bladensburg	MD
408	LEWIS	SALLIE	20	5.00	Ellicott Mills	MD
199	LEWIS	STEWARD	24	10.00	Drainstown	MD
332	LEWIS	STEWARD	24	10.00	Bladensburg	MD
156	LEWIS	THOMAS	21	11.00	Anne Arundel Co.	MD
967	LEWIS	WILLIAM	26	15.00	Carolina Landing	MS
427	LINDSEY	LUCY A.	20	4.00	Maine	NY
968	LIPSCOMB	BARNARD	24	15.00	Carolina Landing	MS
393	LOCKS	CHARLES	12	25.00	Bryantown	MD
1006	LOCKS	CHARLES	26	15.00	Lake Providence	LA
291	LOMAX	MANUR	16	4.00	Aquasco	MD
152	LOMAX	MARGARET	13	.00	Dorchester Co.	MD
150	LOMAX	PAGE	40	10.00	Dorchester Co.	MD
151	LOMAX	TINA	40	5.00	Dorchester Co.	MD
549	LONG	HENRY	28	8.00	Canton	MS
38	LOTSOR*	MONICA	47	8.00	Montgomery Co.	MD
39	LOWE	HENRY	30	10.00	Matthews Store	MD
798	LUCAS	ROBERT	24	15.00	Carolina Landing	MS
95	LUCKLEY	JOHN	30	25.00	Acquia Creek Land.	MD
6	LYON	JOHN	14	5.00	Clearfield Co.	PA
210	MACKEY	JOHN	40	10.00	Montgomery Co.	MD
135	MACON	JOHN	21	15.00	Anne Arundel Co.	MD
143	MALOY	CHARLES	17	.00	Crownsville	MD
18	MANLEY	CHARLES	30	12.00	Albany	NY
19	MANLEY	JENNIE	24	8.00	Albany	NY
836	MANUEL	CHARLES	28	15.00	Carolina Landing	MS
568	MANYOU	JOHN	18	8.00	Canton	MS
432	MARBRY	ANDREW	26	.00	Edgehill	VA
425	MARCH	ELIZABETH	24	5.00	Jessups Cut	MD
524	MARCUS	WILLIAM	15	1.00	Rutland	MD
258	MARKS	JAMES	30	10.00	Allens Fresh	MD
1056	MARSHALL	BENJAMIN	24	15.00	Lake Providence	LA

691	MARSHALL	E.	28	10.00	South River	MD
955	MARSHALL	EDWARD	18	15.00	Carolina Landing	MS
507	MARSHALL	GRANDISON	37	8.33	Millersville	MD
918	MARSHALL	VINCENT	28	15.00	Carolina Landing	MS
741	MARTIN	GEORGE	24	12.00	Helena	AR
391	MARTIN	HENRY	24	6.50	Allens Fresh	MD
1099	MARTIN	PETER	26	.00	Baltimore	MD
459	MASCHAL	WILLIAM	29	12.50	Bay View	MD
506	MASON	GEORGE	13	.00	Millersville	MD
137	MASON	JOHN	41	15.00	Anne Arundel Co.	MD
155	MASON	RICHARD	20	10.00	Somersett	MD
548	MATTHEWS	CHARLES	29	12.00	Canton	MS
497	MATTHEWS	JOHN	52	15.00	Point Lookout	MD
628	MATTHEWS	KING	26	10.00	Port Tobacco	MD
668	MATTHEWS	KING	24	9.00	Port Tobacco	MD
347	MATTON	JOHN	11	5.00	Millersville	MD
172	MAWBRY	CORNELIUS	31	12.00	Baltimore	MD
105	MC COY	JAMES	30	10.00	Howard Co.	MD
1097	MC DOWELL	JOHN	20	.00	Baltimore	MD
1096	MC DOWELL	WILLIAM	23	.00	Baltimore	MD
146	MC GRUDER	ANN	18	6.00	Syracuse	NY
1080	MC GRUDER	CHARLES	20	.00	Philadelphia	PA
1079	MC GRUDER	JOHN	28	.00	Philadelphia	PA
992	MC GUIRE	REBECCA	22	5.00	Egg Harbor	NJ
376	MC LANE	FRED	22	9.17	Aquasco	MD
273	MC LANE	GEORGIANNA	14	2.00	Marriottsville	MD
270	MC LANE	HENRY	38	14.00	Marriottsville	MD
271	MC LANE	LUCY	24	6.00	Marriottsville	MD
272	MC LANE	SALLIE	16	3.00	Marriottsville	MD
355	MERRYMAN	JOHN	18	4.38	Beantown	MD
990	MIDDLETON	ALFRED	14	2.00	Bladensburg	MD
228	MILLER	JAMES H.	20	9.17	Poplar Springs	MD
88	MILLER	MOSES	26	10.00	Hoods Mill	MD
138	MILTON	KASPER	24	15.00	Anne Arundel Co.	MD
214	MINER	RICHARD	29	8.33	Prince Georges Co.	MD
1104	MINES	CHARLES	24	.00	Baltimore	MD
463	MINES*	ROBERT	26	12.00	Vicksburgh	MS
1089	MITCHELL	BOB	26	.00	Philadelphia	PA
209	MITCHELL	GEORGE	19	9.17	Millersville	MD
1038	MITCHELL	HENRY	17	8.00	Lake Providence	LA
93	MITCHELL	JOHN	19	25.00	Acquia Creek Land.	MD
122	MITCHELL	JOSEPH A.	18	10.00	Millersville	MD
410	MITCHELL	MARTIN	9	.00	Millersville	MD
797	MITCHELL	ROBERT	17	11.00	Carolina Landing	MS
643	MOLTON	CORNELIUS	24	9.00	Prince Frederick	MD
59	MOORE	EDWARD	40	.00	Hoods Mill	MD
834	MOORE	JOHN	16	10.00	Carolina Landing	MS
649	MOORE	JULIA	18	4.00	Lincoln	VA
9	MOORE	SOL	39	10.00	Bladensburg	MD
50	MOORE	SYDNEY	22	13.00	Clifton Heights	MD
352	MOORE	SYDNEY	19	6.75	Charlotte Hall	MD
448	MORRIS	HENRY	28	15.00	Cuyahaga	OH
1045	MORRIS	SARAH	20	10.00	Lake Providence	LA
781	MORRIS	WALTER	24	15.00	Carolina Landing	MS
1046	MORRIS	WESLY	24	15.00	Lake Providence	LA
1100	MORRIS	WILLIAM	29	.00	Baltimore	MD
694	MORRISON	ROBERT	36	12.00	Saint Denis	MD

622	MORTIMER	JOHN	28	8.00	Crownsville	MD
567	MORTON	JAMES	29	10.00	Canton	MS
635	MORTON	JOHN W.	29	6.00	Huntingtown	MD
870	MURPHY	CHARLES	35	15.00	Carolina Landing	MS
56	MYERS	WILLIAM	22	.00	Hoods Mill	MD
569	NACTOR	JOHN	19	8.00	Canton	MS
175	NEAL	JOHN	25	10.00	Howard Co.	MD
34	NEAL	SOL	29	10.00	Freedom	MD
139	NELSON	EDWARD	18	10.38	Anne Arundel Co.	MD
1041	NELSON	JACOB	20	15.00	Lake Providence	LA
262	NELSON	JAMES	24	12.00	Relay House	MD
1040	NELSON	JAMES	28	15.00	Lake Providence	LA
808	NELSON	WILLIAM	26	15.00	Carolina Landing	MS
849	NERITT	JAMES	30	15.00	Carolina Landing	MS
853	NEVILLE	MARIA	20	9.00	Carolina Landing	MS
1127	NICHOLS	JOHN	35	.00	Lewiston	ME
200	NICHOLS	RICHARD	26	10.00	Poolesville	MD
184	NORMAN	MADISON	36	.00	Upper Marlboro	MD
1133	NORTON	LEWIS	19	.00	Philadelphia	PA
795	ORTON	JAMES H.	16	9.00	Carolina Landing	MS
925	PAGE	ED	30	15.00	Carolina Landing	MS
187	PALMAN	DRED	28	10.00	Calvert Co.	MD
1060	PALMER	ROBERT	32	15.00	Lake Providence	LA
914	PARKER	CATHERINE	21	4.00	Carolina Landing	MS
75	PARKER	DANIEL	21	.00	Hoods Mill	MD
790	PARKER	EMILY	26	9.00	Carolina Landing	MS
916	PARKER	FRANK	27	15.00	Carolina Landing	MS
842	PARKER	JEFF	28	15.00	Carolina Landing	MS
852	PARKER	JOHN	24	15.00	Carolina Landing	MS
850	PARKER	JOSEPH	27	15.00	Carolina Landing	MS
915	PARKER	LUCY	16	9.00	Carolina Landing	MS
791	PARKER	MARY	6	.00	Carolina Landing	MS
789	PARKER	RICHARD	30	15.00	Carolina Landing	MS
917	PARKER	SALLIE	10	.00	Carolina Landing	MS
912	PARKER	WILLIAM	30	15.00	Carolina Landing	MS
344	PARKS	WILLIAM	26	8.33	Baltimore	MD
379	PATERSON	SANDY	30	9.17	Aquasco	MD
384	PAYNE	ARCHY	28	9.17	Aquasco	MD
979	PAYNE	BEDFORD	24	12.00	Westmoreland Co.	VA
386	PAYNE	HENRY	26	9.17	Aquasco	MD
416	PEABODY	JOHN	24	8.33	Millersville	MD
367	PEARSON	FRANK	22	8.00	Piscataway	MD
832	PENDLETON	GEORGE	16	10.00	Carolina Landing	MS
3	PEOPLES	PAUL	23	10.00	Montgomery Co.	MD
28	PERRY	ALLEN	25	12.00	Hoods Mill	MD
317	PERRY	CLEM	20	8.00	Millersville	MD
29	PERRY	JOHN	16	4.00	Hoods Mill	MD
774	PINDLE	CHARLES	28	15.00	Carolina Landing	MS
329	PLUMMER	ADAM	12	4.25	Millersville	MD
284	POLLARD	LUCINDA	24	3.00	Dunkirk	MD
269	POLLARD	TINA	74	.00	Piscataway	MD
825	PONGSTON*	W.N.	28	10.00	Carolina Landing	MS
249	POPE	GEORGE	46	18.00	Norfolk	VA
621	PRICE	ALBERT	26	10.00	Portsville	MD
265	PRICE	HANNAH	26	4.00	Piscataway	MD
268	PRICE	HESTER	8	.00	Piscataway	MD
167	PRICE	HUGAR*	33	10.00	King George	VA

264	PRICE	JAMES	30	8.00	Piscataway	MD
266	PRICE	MARGARET	15	2.08	Piscataway	MD
267	PRICE	MARIA	9	.00	Piscataway	MD
391	PRICE	WILLIAM	28	6.75	Bryantown	MD
608	PRIOR	TURNER	30	10.00	Savage Station	MD
960	PROSIER	JOHNSON	36	15.00	Carolina Landing	MS
1007	PROSIER	JOHNSON	28	15.00	Lake Providence	LA
823	QUIGGS	ALEX	24	15.00	Carolina Landing	MS
561	QUINCE	WILLIAM	19	8.00	Canton	MS
467	RANSOM	LEWIS	20	12.00	Vicksburgh	MS
1049	RAX*	BENJAMIN	24	15.00	Lake Providence	LA
438	REDD	CHARLES	24	.00	Edgehill	VA
943	REDD	CHARLES	19	15.00	Carolina Landing	MS
570	REDDICK	HENRY	40	10.00	Canton	MS
952	REDRICK	STEPHEN	30	15.00	Carolina Landing	MS
8	REED	ALBERT	30	10.00	Olney	MD
1002	REED	CHARLES	24	15.00	Lake Providence	LA
932	REED	RICHARD	30	15.00	Carolina Landing	MS
589	REED	THOMAS	10	.00	Canton	MS
25	REGANS	ALFRED	25	15.00	Prince Georges Co.	MD
947	REVERARD*	ROLLA	29	15.00	Carolina Landing	MS
5	REYNOLDS	JOHN	22	10.00	Montgomery Co.	MD
7	REYNOLDS	JOHN	18	11.38	Beltsville	MD
201	REYNOLDS	WILSON	21	10.00	Poolesville	MD
680	RICE	FRANK J.	10	.00	Bladensburg	MD
1	RICHARDS	DICK	24	10.00	Montgomery Co	MD
212	RICHARDS	DICK	50	15.00	Brooks Station	MD
641	RICHARDSON	GEORGE	26	8.00	Huntingtown	MD
717	RICHMOND	BUCKUR	24	12.00	Helena	AR
337	RICKS	MADISON	19	8.00	Davidsville	MD
1001	RIDANISH	WILLIAM	21	15.00	Lake Providence	LA
819	RINGOL	ROBERT	18	10.00	Carolina Landing	MS
121	RIVERS	ROLAND	24	10.00	Millersville	MD
679	RNE	PEGGY CLAYBO	30	6.00	Bladensburg	MD
76	ROAN	SCOTT	24	.00	Hoods Mill	MD
377	ROAN	WILLIAM	28	9.17	Aquasco	MD
250	ROBBINS	HENRY	38	9.00	Bryantown	MD
36	ROBERT	WILSON	21	10.00	Woodrind	MD
191	ROBERTSON	JAMES	20	10.00	Anne Arundel Co.	MD
616	ROBERTSON	JOHN	26	7.00	Friendship	MD
709	ROBERTSON	JOHN	21	12.00	Helena	AR
754	ROBERTSON	MINER	30	12.00	Helena	AR
219	ROBINSON	ANNA	28	5.00	Princess Anne	MD
254	ROBINSON	EBEN	20	6.00	Chaptico	MD
220	ROBINSON	FANNIE	6	.00	Princess Anne	MD
572	ROBINSON	HENRY	18	8.00	Canton	MS
663	ROBINSON	HENRY	18	7.00	Newburg	MD
794	ROBINSON	HENRY	22	15.00	Carolina Landing	MS
1069	ROBINSON	HENRY	22	15.00	Lake Providence	LA
886	ROBINSON	JOHN	32	15.00	Carolina Landing	MS
1064	ROBINSON	JOHN	19	15.00	Lake Providence	LA
644	ROBINSON	LAWRENCE	24	9.00	Prince Frederick	MD
940	ROBINSON	NAT	31	15.00	Carolina Landing	MS
373	ROBINSON	ROBERT	30	9.17	Aquasco	MD
708	ROGERS	AARON	18	12.00	Helena	AR
725	ROLLINS	JOHN	19	12.00	Helena	AR
724	ROLLINS	ROBERT	29	12.00	Helena	AR

388	ROSS	MARY	22	2.50	Allens Fresh	MD
389	ROSS	MINNIE	6	.00	Allens Fresh	MD
378	ROSS	THOMAS	20	9.17	Aquasco	MD
931	RUSH	HENRY	27	15.00	Carolina Landing	MS
458	SAMPSON	HENRY	32	12.50	Bay View	MD
1105	SANDERS	RICHARD	21	.00	Baltimore	MD
533	SAUNDERS	BETTY	20	4.00	Huntingtown	MD
23	SAUNDERS	FRANK	21	10.00	Hoods Mill	MD
475	SAUNDERS	JOHN	32	12.00	Vicksburgh	MS
522	SAUNDERS	JOHN	32	8.00	Huntingtown	MD
730	SAUNDERSON	HARRISON	21	12.00	Helena	AR
303	SAVAGE	FANNY	26	6.00	Bealton	MD
302	SAVAGE	WILEY	36	14.00	Bealton	MD
421	SAWYER	JOHN	30	10.00	Little Gunpowder	MD
879	SAWYER	JULIA	28	9.00	Carolina Landing	MS
847	SAWYER	THOMAS	26	15.00	Carolina Landing	MS
696	SAYES	BELFORD	20	12.00	Saint Denis	MD
20	SCOTT	ALBERT	21	10.00	Hoods Mill	MD
186	SCOTT	GEORGE	23	10.00	Darnestown	MD
984	SCOTT	GEORGE	28	10.00	Mt. Vernon	IL
722	SCOTT	JACOB	18	12.00	Helena	AR
430	SCOTT	JOHN	22	.00	Edgehill	VA
963	SCOTT	WILLIAM	26	15.00	Carolina Landing	MS
134	SEDDLES	GEORGE	31	15.00	Anne Arundel Co.	MD
596	SEPHAS	WILLIS	26	8.00	Huntingtown	MD
1042	SERIUS*	THOMAS	29	15.00	Lake Providence	LA
494	SETTLER	TAYLOR	13	4.00	Allens Fresh	MD
392	SHAW	FRANK	16	1.25	Bryantown	MD
881	SHAW	GEORGE H.	26	15.00	Carolina Landing	MS
366	SHELDON	JAMES	24	8.00	Piscataway	MD
711	SHEPERD	GEORGE	26	12.00	Helena	AR
878	SHEPHERD	ANTHONY	26	15.00	Carolina Landing	MS
401	SHOCK	EMILY	19	3.75	Bryantown	MD
998	SHORES	PHILIP	30	15.00	Lake Providence	LA
1005	SHORTER	FRANK	19	15.00	Lake Providence	LA
736	SHORTER	JAMES	26	12.00	Helena	AR
733	SHORTER	KINGSLY	28	12.00	Helena	AR
811	SILLS*	JOHN E.	22	15.00	Carolina Landing	MS
297	SIMS	JAMES	10	.00	Baltimore	MD
610	SIMS	JOHN	26	8.00	Millersville	MD
678	SKINNER	BRUTUS	23	10.00	Arnolds Store	MD
757	SKINNER	ELLIS	28	15.00	Carolina Landing	MS
674	SLADE	CHA	24	10.00	Huntingtown	MD
495	SLAUGHTER	WILLIAM	24	8.00	Crownsville	MD
1047	SMALLWOOD	ARTHUR	28	15.00	Lake Providence	LA
395	SMITH	ALEXANDER	28	7.50	Allens Fresh	MD
723	SMITH	ALEXANDER	40	12.00	Helena	AR
1076	SMITH	ANDERSON	21	.00	Philadelphia	PA
586	SMITH	ANNA	32	.00	Canton	MS
770	SMITH	ANTHONY	28	15.00	Carolina Landing	MS
585	SMITH	BENJAMIN	34	12.00	Canton	MS
587	SMITH	ELLEN	17	.00	Canton	MS
975	SMITH	GEORGE	22	15.00	Carolina Landing	MS
444	SMITH	HENRY	26	12.00	Lehigh	PA
491	SMITH	HENRY	17	12.00	Vicksburgh	MS
861	SMITH	HENRY	21	15.00	Carolina Landing	MS
660	SMITH	JAMES	30	9.00	St. Johnsville	NY

68	SMITH	JOHN	26	12.50	Hoods Mill	MD
78	SMITH	JOHN	29	11.75	Hoods Mill	MD
557	SMITH	JOHN	20	8.00	Canton	MS
664	SMITH	JOHN	26	8.00	Cambridge	MD
556	SMITH	JOHN L.	30	10.00	Canton	MS
92	SMITH	JOSH	21	25.00	Acquia Creek Land.	MD
588	SMITH	MARTHA	15	.00	Canton	MS
1142	SMITH	MARY	17	.00	Philadelphia	PA
154	SMITH	RICHARD	22	12.00	Somersett	MD
1118	SMITH	RICHARD	19	.00	Baltimore	MD
747	SMITH	THOMAS	20	12.00	Helena	AR
227	SMITH	WILLIAM	24	10.00	Montgomery Co.	MD
665	SMITH	WILLIAM	20	12.00	Cambridge	MD
1039	SNIDER	RICHARD	16	8.00	Lake Providence	LA
208	SNOWDEN	CHARLES E.	28	9.17	Millersville	MD
983	SNOWDON	WILLIAM	31	10.00	Allentown	PA
474	SPARKS	HENRY	26	12.00	Vicksburgh	MS
954	SPENCER	KATE	18	9.00	Carolina Landing	MS
889	SPICER	JOSEPH	28	15.00	Carolina Landing	MS
891	SPICER	MARY	21	9.00	Carolina Landing	MS
169	SPILLER	WILLIAM	24	10.00	King George	VA
287	SPRIGGS	JEFF	24	8.00	Port Tobacco	MD
217	SPRIGGS	JEFFERSON	50	11.17	Clarksburgh	MD
400	STARK	WASHINGTON	19	3.75	Bryantown	MD
773	STATEN	DAVID	30	15.00	Carolina Landing	MS
577	STEVENS	STANLEY	36	10.00	Canton	MS
864	STEWARD	THOMAS	20	15.00	Carolina Landing	MS
822	STEWART	WILLIAM	30	15.00	Carolina Landing	MS
37	STRAWDER	HENRY	15	1.00	Lockeysville	MD
73	STROKES	DAVID	26	.00	Hoods Mill	MD
654	TALIAFERRO	EASTER	26	4.00	Rockville	MD
653	TALIAFERRO	WILLIAM	30	10.00	Rockville	MD
966	TAYLOR	ADALAIDE	28	9.00	Carolina Landing	MS
229	TAYLOR	AUGUSTUS	18	1.50	Howard Co.	MD
698	TAYLOR	BEVERLY	28	12.00	Helena	AR
483	TAYLOR	FRANK	20	12.00	Vicksburgh	MS
938	TAYLOR	JAMES	27	15.00	Carolina Landing	MS
513	TAYLOR	JOHN	21	8.33	Occuquan	VA
207	TAYLOR	JOHN R.	30	9.17	Aquasco	MD
948	TAYLOR	JOSEPH	30	15.00	Carolina Landing	MS
26	TAYLOR	PHILIP	21	10.00	Prince Georges Co.	MD
562	TAYLOR	ROBERT	40	10.00	Canton	MS
331	TAYLOR	SPENCER	25	8.00	Davidsville	MD
856	TAYLOR	SPENCER	20	15.00	Carolina Landing	MS
251	TAYLOR	TIMOTHY	16	7.08	Bryantown	MD
462	TAYLOR	W.H.	24	12.00	Vicksburgh	MS
417	TAYLOR	ZACK	14	5.00	Luckburgh	PA
126	TEMPLE	EDWARD	16	8.00	Millersville	MD
953	TENNISON	ALBERT	27	15.00	Carolina Landing	MS
638	TERRIU*	ALBERT	20	9.00	Huntingtown	MD
745	TERRY	WILLIAM	23	15.00	Helena	AR
488	THOMAS	BENJAMIN	20	12.00	Vicksburgh	MS
149	THOMAS	CAROLINE	18	5.00	Howard Co.	MD
489	THOMAS	EDWARD	26	12.00	Vicksburgh	MS
70	THOMAS	GEORGE	28	.00	Hoods Mill	MD
482	THOMAS	JAMES	21	12.00	Vicksburgh	MS
471	THOMAS	JOHN	28	12.00	Vicksburgh	MS

552	THOMAS	JOHN	27	10.00	Canton	MS
776	THOMAS	JOHN	28	15.00	Carolina Landing	MS
1037	THOMAS	JOHN	24	15.00	Lake Providence	LA
1102	THOMAS	JOHN	20	.00	Baltimore	MD
962	THOMAS	JOSEPH	41	15.00	Carolina Landing	MS
300	THOMAS	LEWIS	28	10.00	Allens Fresh	MD
658	THOMAS	SAMPSON	26	9.00	Millersville	MD
15	THOMAS	SAMUEL	26	10.00	Hoods Mill	MD
286	THOMAS	THOMAS	26	8.00	Port Tobacco	MD
487	THOMAS	WILLIAM	24	12.00	Vicksburgh	MS
764	THOMAS	WILLIAM	30	15.00	Carolina Landing	MS
1009	THOMAS	WILLIAM	27	15.00	Lake Providence	LA
816	THOMAS, 2ND	JOHN	26	15.00	Carolina Landing	MS
221	THOMPSON	ANDREW	30	10.00	Queenstown	MD
222	THOMPSON	ELLEN	20	.00	Queenstown	MD
1054	THOMPSON	JOHN	28	15.00	Lake Providence	LA
550	THOMPSON	JOSEPH	15	6.00	Canton	MS
601	THOMPSON	MARTIN	24	8.00	Millersville	MD
338	THOMPSON	ROBERT	24	9.17	Davidsville	MD
1122	THORNTON	ALLEN	21	.00	Lewiston	ME
1028	THORNTON	MOSES	30	15.00	Lake Providence	LA
820	THORNTON	NAT	27	15.00	Carolina Landing	MS
1124	THORNTON	SARAH	24	.00	Lewiston	ME
1123	THORNTON	WILLIAM	18	.00	Lewiston	ME
185	TOLSON*	WILLIAM	31	.00	Upper Marlboro	MD
1143	TOMLINSON*	MARY	19	.00	Philadelphia	PA
530	TOWNS	ROBERT	24	8.00	Friendship	MD
485	TRAVERSE	AUSTIN	20	12.00	Vicksburgh	MS
705	TRAVERSE	AUSTIN	30	12.00	Helena	AR
22	TRUSTY	JESS	19	8.00	Hoods Mill	MD
1071	TRUTON*	WILLIAM	20	15.00	Lake Providence	LA
85	TUCKER	ANN	7	.00	Marriottsville	MD
204	TUCKER	DAVID	40	12.00	Anne Arundel Co.	MD
82	TUCKER	JOHN	31	12.00	Marriottsville	MD
84	TUCKER	JOHN	9	.00	Marriottsville	MD
83	TUCKER	MARY	30	5.00	Marriottsville	MD
205	TUCKER	MARY	29	1.75	Anne Arundel Co.	MD
86	TUCKER	SARAH	4	.00	Marriottsville	MD
385	TUCKER	WILLIAM	31	9.17	Aquasco	MD
450	TUCKER	WILLIAM	22	12.00	Cleveland	OH
632	TUCKER	WILLIAM	24	9.00	Allens Fresh	MD
102	TURNER	DENNIS	27	15.00	Lake Providence	LA
65	TURNER	JOHN	25	10.00	Davidsonville	MD
442	TURNER	SAMUEL	30	10.00	Savage	MD
594	TYLER	BAILY	30	10.00	Canton	MS
80	TYLER	JAMES	14	1.00	Warfield	IN
609	TYLER	JANE	20	3.00	Millersville	MD
651	TYLER	JANE	14	4.00	Lincoln	VA
771	UPERHARK	CHELSEY	28	9.00	Carolina Landing	MS
815	VALENTINE	HORACE	23	15.00	Carolina Landing	MS
1033	VAUGHN	ABRAM	24	24.00	Lake Providence	LA
1062	VAUGHN	ALEX	28	15.00	Lake Providence	LA
1029	VAUGHN	MARY	20	10.00	Lake Providence	LA
11	VENABLE	HENRY	21	10.00	Hoods Mill	MD
833	VIRGINIA	ELEANOR	17	8.00	Carolina Landing	MS
769	WADDY	MARY	6	.00	Carolina Landing	MS
768	WADDY	MRS. SMITH	30	9.00	Carolina Landing	MS

767	WADDY	SMITH	50	15.00	Carolina Landing	MS
961	WADE	HENRY	40	15.00	Carolina Landing	MS
1109	WADSWORTH	HENRY	18	.00	Baltimore	MD
1018	WALKER	ALFRED	26	15.00	Lake Providence	LA
469	WALKER	BENJAMIN	24	12.00	Vicksburgh	MS
24	WALKER	FRANK	18	8.00	Hoods Mill	MD
875	WARD	FRED	20	15.00	Carolina Landing	MS
1035	WARD	HAWLEY	19	12.00	Lake Providence	LA
905	WARDEN	SAMUEL	24	15.00	Carolina Landing	MS
1061	WARNER	HENRY	31	15.00	Lake Providence	LA
753	WARREN	HENRY	20	12.00	Helena	AR
890	WARREN	LORRY	30	15.00	Carolina Landing	MS
509	WASHINGTON	ANNA	28	4.00	Rutland	IL
180	WASHINGTON	ARGUS	19	.00	Upper Marlboro	MD
956	WASHINGTON	BETTIE	24	9.00	Carolina Landing	MS
402	WASHINGTON	EMILY	20	5.00	Millersville	MD
278	WASHINGTON	EVAN	4	.00	Prince Georges Co.	MD
16	WASHINGTON	GEORGE	32	10.00	Hoods Mill	MD
159	WASHINGTON	GEORGE	26	9.17	Millersville	MD
374	WASHINGTON	GEORGE	28	9.17	Aquasco	MD
800	WASHINGTON	GEORGE	28	15.00	Carolina Landing	MS
888	WASHINGTON	HRNTY	40	15.00	Carolina Landing	MS
455	WASHINGTON	JOHN	30	12.00	Princeton	NJ
510	WASHINGTON	NANNIE	12	.00	Rutland	IL
511	WASHINGTON	ROBERT	4	.00	Rutland	IL
508	WASHINGTON	WILLIAM	34	7.00	Rutland	IL
860	WASHINGTON	GEORGE	28	15.00	Carolina Landing	MS
1094	WATERS	HENRY	23	.00	Philadelphia	PA
671	WATERS	WILLIAM H.	21	9.00	Port Tobacco	MD
1008	WATKINS	JOHN	20	15.00	Lake Providence	LA
158	WATKINS	LEONARD	53	9.17	Millersville	MD
611	WATKINS	LEWIS	14	5.00	Snickersville	VA
763	WATSON	GEORGE	19	15.00	Carolina Landing	MS
1070	WATSON	HENRY	26	15.00	Lake Providence	LA
1051	WATSON	ROBERT	30	15.00	Lake Providence	LA
600	WATTS	LEWIS	28	12.00	Millersville	MD
900	WEBER	S.	30	15.00	Carolina Landing	MS
157	WEBSTER	ANDREW	54	9.17	Millersville	MD
835	WELLINGTON	NELSON	24	15.00	Carolina Landing	MS
120	WELLS	ELIZA	1	.00	Glennell	MD
118	WELLS	NELSON	39	10.00	Glennell	MD
119	WELLS	PATSEY	29	.00	Glennell	MD
634	WEST	JAMES	29	15.00	Hyattsville	MD
164	WESTERLY	HAM	21	20.00	Waterford	PA
807	WHEELER	HENRY	27	15.00	Carolina Landing	MS
817	WHIMS	ROBERT	22	15.00	Carolina Landing	MS
490	WHITE	ALFRED	19	12.00	Vicksburgh	MS
873	WHITE	ANDERSON	31	15.00	Carolina Landing	MS
409	WHITE	ANNA	19	3.33	Bryantown	MD
441	WHITE	ANNAPOLIS	28	10.00	Arnoldtown	MD
275	WHITE	HARRIETTE	30	3.00	Prince Georges Co.	MD
277	WHITE	JAMES	8	.00	Prince Georges Co.	MD
276	WHITE	JOHN	10	.00	Prince Georges Co.	MD
1093	WHITE	LEWIS	28	.00	Philadelphia	PA
127	WHITE	NED	19	15.00	Monocacy*	MD
383	WHITNEY	JAMES	32	9.17	Aquasco	MD
601	WICKER	JAMES	20	8.00	Millersville	MD

592	WIGGINS	ISAIAH	40	10.00	Canton	MS
363	WILLIAMS	BENJAMIN	14	3.33	Silver Creek	MD
988	WILLIAMS	BENJAMIN	18	7.00	Allentown	PA
1066	WILLIAMS	CHARLES	24	15.00	Lake Providence	LA
406	WILLIAMS	DELIA	19	5.00	West River	MD
476	WILLIAMS	DENNIS	24	12.00	Vicksburgh	MS
189	WILLIAMS	EDWARD	28	10.00	Anne Arundel Co.	MD
190	WILLIAMS	ELLEN	18	8.00	Anne Arundel Co.	MD
1130	WILLIAMS	EMILY	27	.00	Lewiston	ME
239	WILLIAMS	EMMA	24	5.00	Hoopersville	MD
470	WILLIAMS	HENRY	25	12.00	Vicksburgh	MS
1092	WILLIAMS	ISAAC	21	.00	Philadelphia	PA
496	WILLIAMS	JAMES	16	4.25	Crownsville	MD
659	WILLIAMS	JAMES	24	9.00	Millersvills	MD
1114	WILLIAMS	JERRY	23	.00	Baltimore	MD
1116	WILLIAMS	JERRY	21	.00	Baltimore	MD
98	WILLIAMS	JOHN	25	35.00	Acquia Creek Land.	MD
484	WILLIAMS	JOHN	18	12.00	Vicksburgh	MS
1068	WILLIAMS	JOHN	27	15.00	Lake Providence	LA
1087	WILLIAMS	JOHN	28	.00	Philadelphia	PA
772	WILLIAMS	JOHN H.	29	15.00	Carolina Landing	MS
306	WILLIAMS	JOHN W.	24	8.00	West River	MD
729	WILLIAMS	JOHN W.	24	12.00	Helena	AR
1131	WILLIAMS	LEMUEL	21	.00	Lewiston	ME
604	WILLIAMS	PARKER	28	8.00	Rutland	MD
716	WILLIAMS	STEPHEN	21	12.00	Helena	AR
174	WILLIAMS	THOMAS	29	10.00	Howard Co.	MD
902	WILLIAMS	THOMAS	21	15.00	Carolina Landing	MS
178	WILLIAMS	ULMSTED*	26	.00	Upper Marlboro	MD
468	WILLIAMSON	CHARLES	23	12.00	Vicksburgh	MS
348	WILLIAMSON	FRANK	12	5.00	Millersville	MD
666	WILLIS	NELSON	23	10.00	Beltsville	MD
672	WILSON	HENRY	26	9.00	Port Tobacco	MD
454	WILSON	JEFF	28	12.00	Princeton	NJ
218	WILSON	JOHN	15	5.00	Prince Georges Co.	MD
743	WILSON	PARM	36	12.00	Helena	AR
739	WILSON	REUBEN	21	12.00	Helena	AR
96	WILSON	ROBERT	21	25.00	Acquia Creek Land.	MD
466	WILSON	ROBERT	19	12.00	Vicksburgh	MS
247	WILSON	SAMUEL	24	18.00	Sykesville	MD
1101	WILSON	WILLIAM	28	.00	Baltimore	MD
422	WINFIELD	HARRIETTE	20	5.00	Montgomery Co.	MD
563	WINFIELD	ROBERT	28	10.00	Canton	MS
906	WINFIELD	WILLIAM	28	15.00	Carolina Landing	MS
128	WINTERS	DAVID	20	10.00	Monocacy*	MD
970	WISE	BENJAMIN	36	15.00	Carolina Landing	MS
43	WISE	HENRY	18	8.00	Millersville	MD
707	WITTED*	JOSEPH	29	12.00	Helena	AR
964	WOOD	JOHN	24	15.00	Carolina Landing	MS
639	WOODEN	HENRY	26	9.00	Huntingtown	MD
818	WOOTON	ANDREW	28	15.00	Carolina Landing	MS
740	WORKALL	JOHN	31	12.00	Helena	AR
760	WORMLEY*	WILSON	30	.00	Carolina Landing	MS
30	WORTHAM	WADDY	19	10.00	Hoods Mill	MD
308	WRIGHT	HARRY	16	1.00	West River	MD
838	WRIGHT	ISRAEL	24	15.00	Carolina Landing	MS
999	WRIGHT	ISRAEL	28	15.00	Lake Providence	LA

735	WRIGHT	PAGE	30	12.00	Helena	AR
913	WRIGHT*	KRIS	16	8.00	Carolina Landing	MS
802	YOUNG	PRISCILLA	18	9.00	Carolina Landing	MS
618	YOUNG	SOL	24	10.00	Hillsboro	VA
486	YOUNG	WILLIAM	18	12.00	Vicksburgh	MS
843	ZARRETT*	TERI	26	15.00	Carolina Landing	MS
560	ZIMMERMAN	EPHRAIM	29	10.00	Canton	MS

INDEX THREE

AFRICAN AMERICANS SENT OUT FROM THE DISTRICT OF COLUMBIA UNDER WORK CONTRACTS APPROVED BY THE FREEDMEN'S BUREAU

A Presidential Order issued April 24, 1866, required that the Assistant Commissioner of the District of Columbia submit a report of African Americans sent to work under contracts approved by the Freedmen's Bureau. In this index, Column 1 lists the consecutive number that was assigned to the individual as the name was listed on the original report.

Sex of each person is not given in this index. Females were paid less than $10.00. Where the sex is not obvious by the first name, the rate of pay should distinguish whether the individual was a male or a female.

In many instances, the rate of pay is shown as "$0.00." Those who were not paid a monthly wage were compensated with room, board, schooling, and medical attention, or were paid for their production of cords of wood and other like services.

Inasmuch as some individuals were sent out to work on more than one contract, they may be listed more than once.

Although the length of each contract was given in the report, the beginning dates of the contracts were not included in the report.